Four Futures

The Jacobin series features short interrogations of politics, economics, and culture from a socialist perspective, as an avenue to radical political practice. The books offer critical analysis and engagement with the history and ideas of the Left in an accessible format.

The series is a collaboration between Verso Books and *Jacobin* magazine, which is published quarterly in print and online at jacobinmag.com.

Other titles in this series available from Verso Books:

The New Prophets of Capital by Nicole Aschoff
Playing the Whore by Melissa Gira Grant
Utopia or Bust by Benjamin Kunkel
Strike for America by Micah Uetricht
Class War by Megan Erickson

Four Futures

Visions of the World After Capitalism

PETER FRASE

VERSO

London • New York

This edition first published by Verso 2016
© Peter Frase 2016

5 7 9 10 8 6 4

Verso
UK: 6 Meard Street, London W1F 0EG
US: 20 Jay Street, Suite 1010, Brooklyn, NY 11201
versobooks.com

Verso is the imprint of New Left Books

ISBN-13: 978-1-78168-813-7
ISBN-13: 978-1-78168-815-1 (US EBK)
ISBN-13: 978-1-78168-814-4 (UK EBK)

British Library Cataloguing in Publication Data
A catalogue record for this book is available from the British Library

Library of Congress Cataloging-in-Publication Data
Names: Frase, Peter, author.
Title: Four futures : visions of the world after capitalism / by Peter Frase.
Description: Brooklyn, NY : Verso, 2016. | Includes bibliographical
references and index.
Identifiers: LCCN 2016023756 (print) | LCCN 2016036476 (ebook) | ISBN
9781781688137 (pbk. : alk. paper) | ISBN 9781781688151
Subjects: LCSH: Economics. | Economic forecasting. | Economic history. |
Capitalism.
Classification: LCC HB72 .F6775 2016 (print) | LCC HB72 (ebook) | DDC
330--dc23
LC record available at https://lccn.loc.gov/2016023756

Typeset in Fournier by Hewer Text UK Ltd, Edinburgh, Scotland
Printed and bound by CPI Group (UK) Ltd, Croydon, CR0 4YY

CONTENTS

INTRODUCTION:
TECHNOLOGY AND ECOLOGY
AS APOCALYPSE AND UTOPIA

Two specters are haunting Earth in the twenty-first century: the specters of ecological catastrophe and automation.

In 2013, a US government observatory recorded that global concentration of atmospheric carbon dioxide had reached 400 parts per million for the first time in recorded history.[1] This threshold, which the Earth had not passed in as many as 3 million years, heralds accelerating climate change over the coming century. The Intergovernmental Panel on Climate Change predicts diminishing sea ice, acidification of the oceans, and increasing frequency of droughts and extreme storm events.[2]

---

1 National Oceanic and Atmospheric Administration, "Trends in Atmospheric Carbon Dioxide," ESRL.NOAA.gov, 2014.
2 Thomas F. Stocker et al., "Climate Change 2013: The Physical Science Basis," Intergovernmental Panel on Climate Change, Working Group I Contribution to the Fifth Assessment Report of the Intergovernmental Panel on Climate Change, New York: Cambridge University Press, 2013.

At the same time, news of technological breakthroughs in the context of high unemployment and stagnant wages has produced anxious warnings about the effects of automation on the future of work. In early 2014, Massachusetts Institute of Technology professors Erik Brynjolfsson and Andrew McAfee published *The Second Machine Age: Work, Progress, and Prosperity in a Time of Brilliant Technologies*.[3] They surveyed a future in which computer and robotics technology replaces human labor not just in traditional domains such as agriculture and manufacturing, but also in sectors ranging from medicine and law to transportation. At Oxford University, a research unit released a widely publicized report estimating that nearly half the jobs in the United States today are vulnerable to computerization.[4]

These twin anxieties are in many ways diametrical opposites. The fear of climate change is a fear of having too little: it anticipates a scarcity of natural resources, the loss of agricultural land and habitable environments—and ultimately the demise of an Earth that can support human life. The fear of automation is, perversely, a fear of too *much*: a fully robotized economy that produces so much, with so little human labor, that there is no longer any need for workers. Can we really be facing a crisis of scarcity and a crisis of abundance at the same time?

---

3   Erik Brynjolfsson and Andrew McAfee, *The Second Machine Age: Work, Progress, and Prosperity in a Time of Brilliant Technologies*, New York: W. W. Norton, 2014.

4   Carl Benedikt Frey and Michael A. Osborne, "The Future of Employment: How Susceptible Are Jobs to Computerisation?," OxfordMartin.ox.ac.uk, 2013.

The argument of this book is that we are in fact facing such a contradictory dual crisis. And it is the interaction of these two dynamics that makes our historical moment so volatile and uncertain, full of both promise and danger. In the chapters that follow, I will attempt to sketch some of the possible interactions between these two dynamics.

First, however, I need to lay out the contours of current debates over automation and climate change.

Rise of the Robots

"Welcome Robot Overlords," reads a feature headline published in 2013 by *Mother Jones* magazine, "Please Don't Fire Us?"[5] The article, by liberal pundit Kevin Drum, exemplifies a raft of coverage in recent years, surveying the rapid spread of automation and computerization throughout every part of the economy. These stories tend to veer between wonder and dread at the possibilities of all this new gadgetry. In stories like Drum's, rapid progress in automation heralds the possibility of a world with a better quality of life and more leisure time for all; but alternatively, it heralds mass unemployment and the continued enrichment of the 1 percent.

This is not a new tension by any means. The folk tale of John Henry and the steam hammer, which originated in the nineteenth century, describes a railroad worker who tries to

---

5   Kevin Drum, "Welcome, Robot Overlords. Please Don't Fire Us?," *Mother Jones*, May/June 2013.

race against a steel powered drill and wins—only to drop dead from the effort. But several factors have come together to accentuate worries about technology and its effect on labor. The persistently weak post-recession labor market has produced a generalized background anxiety about job loss. Automation and computerization are beginning to reach into professional and creative industries that long seemed immune, threatening the jobs of the very journalists who cover these issues. And the pace of change at least seems, to many, to be faster than ever.

The "second machine age" is a concept promoted by Brynjolfsson and McAfee. In their book of the same name, they argue that just as the first machine age—the Industrial Revolution—replaced human muscle with machine power, computerization is allowing us to greatly magnify, or even replace, "the ability to use our brains to understand and shape our environments."[6] In that book and its predecessor, *Race Against the Machine*, Brynjolfsson and McAfee argue that computers and robots are rapidly permeating every part of the economy, displacing labor from high- and low-skill functions alike. Central to their view is the processing of much of the world into digital information, with everything from books and music to street networks now available in a form that can be copied and transmitted around the world instantly and nearly for free.

The applications that this kind of data enables are enormously varied, especially in combination with advances in

---

6   Brynjolfsson and McAfee, *The Second Machine Age*, pp. 7–8.

physical-world robotics and sensing. In a widely cited study using a detailed analysis of different occupations produced by the US Department of Labor, Oxford University researchers Carl Benedikt Frey and Michael A. Osborne speculated that 47 percent of current US employment is susceptible to computerization thanks to current technological developments.[7] Stuart Elliott at the Organisation for Economic Co-operation and Development uses the same source data but a different approach over a longer time frame and suggested that the figure could be as high as 80 percent. These figures are the result of both subjective classifying decisions and complex quantitative methodology, so it would be a mistake to put too much faith in any exact number. Nevertheless, it should be clear that the possibility of rapid further automation in the near future is very real.

Brynjolfsson and McAfee are perhaps the best-known prophets of rapid automation, but their work fits into an exploding genre. Software entrepreneur Martin Ford, for example, explores similar terrain in his 2015 work *Rise of the Robots*.[8] He relies on much of the same literature and reaches many of the same conclusions about the pace of automation. His conclusions are somewhat more radical—a guaranteed universal basic income, which will be discussed later in this book, occupies a place of prominence; much of the rival literature, by contrast, offers little more than bromides about education.

---

7   Frey and Osborne, "The Future of Employment."
8   Martin Ford, *Rise of the Robots: Technology and the Threat of a Jobless Future,* New York: Basic Books, 2015.

That many people are writing about rapid and socially dislocating automation doesn't mean that it's an imminent reality. As I noted above, anxiety about labor-saving technology is actually a constant through the whole history of capitalism. But we do see many indications that we now have the *possibility*—although not necessarily the reality—of drastically reducing the need for human labor. A few examples will demonstrate the diverse areas in which human labor is being reduced or eliminated entirely.

In 2011, IBM made headlines with its Watson supercomputer, which successfully competed and won against human competitors on the game show *Jeopardy*. Although this feat was a somewhat frivolous publicity stunt, it also demonstrated Watson's suitability for other, more valuable tasks. The technology is already being tested to assist doctors in processing the enormous volume of medical literature to better diagnose patients, which in fact was the system's original purpose. But it is also being released as the "Watson Engagement Advisor," which is intended for customer service and technical support applications. By responding to free-form natural language queries from users, this software could potentially replace the call center workers (many in places like India) who currently perform this work. The review of legal documents, an extremely time-consuming process traditionally performed by legions of junior lawyers, is another promising application of the technology.

Another area of rapid advance is robotics, the interaction of machinery with the physical world. Over the twentieth century, great advances were made in the development of large-scale industrial robots, of the sort that could operate a car assembly line. But only recently have they begun to challenge the areas in which humans excel: fine-grained motor skills and the navigation of a complex physical terrain. The US Department of Defense is now developing computer-controlled sewing machines so as to avoid sourcing its uniforms from China.⁹ Until just the past few years, self-driving cars were regarded as well beyond the scope of our technical ability. Now the combination of sensor technology and comprehensive map databases is making it a reality in such projects as the Google self-driving fleet. Meanwhile a company called Locus Robotics has launched a robot that can process orders in giant warehouses, potentially replacing the workers for Amazon and other companies who currently toil in often brutal conditions.¹⁰

Automation continues to proceed even in agriculture, which once consumed the largest share of human labor but now makes up a tiny fraction of employment, especially in the United States and other rich countries. In California, changing Mexican economic conditions and border crackdowns have led to labor shortages. This has spurred farmers to invest in new machinery that can take on even delicate tasks like fruit harvesting, which have until now required the

9 Katie Drummond, "Clothes Will Sew Themselves in Darpa's Sweat-Free Sweatshops," Wired.com, June 6, 2012.
10 Leanna Garfield, "These Warehouse Robots Can Boost Productivity by 800%," TechInsider.io, February 26, 2016.

precision of a human hand.[11] This development illustrates a recurrent capitalist dynamic: as workers become more powerful and better paid, the pressure on capitalists to automate increases. When there is a huge pool of low wage migrant farm labor, a $100,000 fruit picker looks like a wasteful indulgence. But when workers are scarce and can command better wages, the incentive to replace them with machinery is intensified.

The trend toward automation runs through the entire history of capitalism. In recent years it was muted and somewhat disguised, because of the enormous injection of cheap labor that global capitalism received after the collapse of the Soviet Union and the turn toward capitalism in China. But now even Chinese companies are facing labor shortages and looking to new ways of automating and robotizing.

Innumerable further examples can be produced. Robot anesthesiologists to replace physicians. A hamburger-making machine that can replace the staff of a McDonald's. Large-scale 3-D printers that can turn out entire houses within a day. Each week brings strange new things.

Automation is liable to move beyond even this, into the oldest and most fundamental form of women's labor. In the 1970s, the radical feminist theorist Shulamith Firestone called for growing babies in artificial wombs, as a way to liberate women from their dominated position in the

---

11   Ilan Brat, "Robots Step into New Planting, Harvesting Roles," *Wall Street Journal*, April 23, 2015.

relations of reproduction.[12] Fanciful at the time, such technologies are becoming a reality today. Japanese scientists have successfully birthed goats from artificial wombs and grown human embryos for up to ten days. Further work on applying this technology to human babies is now as much restricted by law as science; Japan prohibits growing human embryos artificially for longer than fourteen days.[13] Many women find such a prospect off-putting and welcome the experience of carrying a child. But surely many others would prefer to be liberated from the obligation.

Most of this book will take for granted the premise of the automation optimists, that within as little as a few decades we could live in a *Star Trek*–like world where, as Kevin Drum put it in *Mother Jones*, "robots can do everything humans can do, and they do it uncomplainingly, 24 hours a day," and "scarcity of ordinary consumer goods is a thing of the past."[14] Such claims are likely to be hyperbole, which for the purposes of this book is fine: my approach is deliberately hyperbolic, sketching out simplified ideal types to illustrate fundamental principles. It's not important that absolutely *everything* will be done by robots, only that a large amount of the labor currently done by humans is in the process of being automated away.

---

12   Shulamith Firestone, *The Dialectic of Sex: The Case for Feminist Revolution*, New York: Farrar, Straus and Giroux, 1970.
13   Soraya Chemaly, "What Do Artificial Wombs Mean for Women?" Rewire.news, February 23, 2012.
14   Drum, "Welcome Robot Overlords."

But there remains much controversy over just how fast automation can proceed and what processes will be susceptible to it. So before delving into the possible social consequences of that process, I will sketch out some of the recent, rapid developments in the so-called "second machine age" we live in. This is a sequel to—or, as some see it, merely an extension of—the first machine age of large-scale industrial automation.

Fear of a Mechanical Planet

Objections to the predictions and fears of wide-ranging automation fall into three broad categories. Some argue that reports of new technology are overhyped and overblown and that we are a long way from truly being able to replace human labor in most fields. Others, following a traditional argument from mainstream economics, contend that past episodes of rapid productivity growth have simply opened up new kinds of work and new jobs, not led to massive unemployment, and that this time will be no different. Finally, some on the Left see an obsessive focus on futuristic automation scenarios as a distraction from more pressing political tasks such as government investment and stimulus and improved wages and conditions in the workplace.

REPORTS OF LABOR'S DEMISE: GREATLY EXAGGERATED?

Those who believe that technology is given exaggerated significance usually point to the published statistics on productivity growth. A large-scale adoption of robots and

machinery ought to show up as a rapid increase in the statistics that measure the productivity of labor—that is, the
amount of output that can be generated per worker. But in
fact, the rate of productivity growth in recent years has been
relatively low. In the United States, the Bureau of Labor
Statistics reports that from 2007 to 2014, the annual rate of
change was only 1.4 percent. That's a pace lower than at any
time since the 1970s and half what was seen during the postwar boom years.

This leads some to argue that the anecdotal accounts of
great breakthroughs in robotics and computation are misleading, because they aren't actually being translated into
economic results. The economists Tyler Cowen and Robert
Gordon are most closely associated with this view.[15] Doug
Henwood, of the *Left Business Observer*, makes a similar case
from the Left.[16]

For more conservative economists like Cowen and
Gordon, the problem is largely technical. The new technologies aren't really all that great, at least from an economic
perspective, compared to breakthroughs like electricity or
the internal combustion engine. We've picked the "low-hanging
fruit," in Cowen's terms, and unless we find some more we're
doomed to slow growth for the foreseeable future.

15 Tyler Cowen, *The Great Stagnation: How America Ate All the
Low-Hanging Fruit of Modern History, Got Sick, and Will (Eventually) Feel
Better*, New York: Penguin, 2011; Robert J. Gordon, "Is U.S. Economic
Growth Over? Faltering Innovation Confronts the Six Headwinds,"
National Bureau of Economic Research Working Paper Series, Cambridge,
MA: National Bureau of Economic Research, August 2012.
16 Doug Henwood, "Workers: No Longer Needed?" Lbo-News.com,
2015.

Left critics, like Henwood and Dean Baker of the Center for Economic and Policy Research, locate our problems not in technology, but in policy. For them, blaming the weak economic recovery after the 2008 recession on automation is a distraction from the real issue, which is that government policy has not been sufficiently focused on fiscal stimulus and job creation, thus preventing the economy from reaching full employment. Worries about robots are, from this point of view, both counter-factual (because productivity growth is low) and politically reactionary.

But others, including Brynjolfsson and McAfee, argue that even if no great fundamental breakthroughs are on the horizon, there is much to be gained from refining and recombining the breakthroughs we have already seen. This is a common historical pattern; many new techniques that were discovered during the Great Depression, for example, weren't economically fully exploited until the postwar boom. Moreover, even those changes that don't get reflected numerically in the Gross Domestic Product can still contribute to our social wealth—like the huge volume of information available freely and rapidly on the Internet, which has greatly increased my efficiency in writing this book.

To leftist critics of the automation narrative, we can offer a more complex answer: their analysis is narrowly correct but doesn't look far enough ahead. This is because the recent trends in productivity can also be read as reflections of a curious tension between the economy's short-term equilibrium and its long-term potential.

The first two recessions of the twenty-first century led to weak recoveries, characterized by stagnant wages and high unemployment. In that context, the existence of a large pool of unemployed and low-wage workers operates as a disincentive for employers to automate. After all, why replace a worker with a robot, if the worker is cheaper? But a corollary to this principle is that, if wages begin to rise and labor markets tighten, employers will start to turn to the new technologies that are currently being developed, rather than pay the cost of additional labor. As I argue in the following sections, the real impediments to tight labor markets are currently political, not technological.

AUTOMATION'S ETERNAL RETURN

Mainstream economists have for generations made the same argument about the supposed danger that automation poses to labor. If some jobs are automated, they argue, labor is freed up for other, new, and perhaps better kinds of work. They point to agriculture, which once occupied most of the workforce but now occupies only about 2 percent of it in a country like the United States. The decline of agricultural employment freed up workers who would go into the factories and make up the great industrial manufacturing economy of the mid-twentieth century. And the subsequent automation and offshoring of manufacturing, in turn, led to the boom in the service sector.

Why, then, should today be any different? If a robot takes your job, something else will surely be on the horizon. Supporters of this position can point to previous waves of anxiety about automation, such as the one in the 1990s that produced works like Jeremy Rifkin's *The End of Work* and Stanley Aronowitz and Bill DeFazio's *The Jobless Future*.[17] As early as 1948, the mathematician and cyberneticist Norbert Weiner warned in his book *Cybernetics* that in the "second, cybernetic industrial revolution," we were approaching a society in which "the average human being of mediocre attainments or less has nothing to sell that it is worth anyone's money to buy."[18] While many jobs have indeed been lost to automation, and jobless rates have risen and fallen with the business cycle, the social crisis of extreme mass unemployment, which many of these authors anticipated, has failed to arrive.

Of course, this is the kind of argument that can only be made from a great academic height, while ignoring the pain and disruption caused to actual workers who are displaced, whether or not they can eventually find new work. And even some in the mainstream suspect that, perhaps, this time really is different. Nobel Prize–winner and *New York Times* columnist Paul Krugman is perhaps the most prominent person to give voice to these doubts.[19] But the deeper problem with the traditional analysis is that it poses the

17   Jeremy Rifkin, *The End of Work: The Decline of the Global Labor Force and the Dawn of the Post-Market Era*, New York: Putnam, 1995; Stanley Aronowitz and William DiFazio, *The Jobless Future: Sci-Tech and the Dogma of Work*, Minneapolis: University of Minnesota Press, 1994.

18   Norbert Wiener, *Cybernetics: Or Control and Communication in the Animal and the Machine*, Cambridge, MA: MIT Press, 1948, p. 28.

19   Paul Krugman, "Sympathy for the Luddites," *New York Times*, June 14, 2013.

process as a scientific inevitability when it is actually a social and political choice.

Today, most labor struggles turn on increasing wages and benefits or improving working conditions. But until the time of the Great Depression in the 1930s, socialist and labor movements struggled for, and won, progressive reductions in the length of the working day as well. In the nineteenth century, the ten-hour-day movement gave way to the eight-hour-day movement. Even in the 1930s, the American Federation of Labor supported a law to reduce the work week to thirty hours. But after World War II, for a variety of reasons, work reduction gradually disappeared from labor's agenda. The forty-hour (or more) week was taken for granted, and the question became merely how well it would be compensated.

This would have surprised the economist John Maynard Keynes, who speculated in the 1930s that people in our time would work as little as fifteen hours per week. That would mean working less than a third of the forty-hour work week that is still widely considered to be the standard. And yet productivity since Keynes's time has more than tripled, so it would have been possible to take that growth in the form of free time for the masses. This didn't happen, not because it isn't technically possible, but because of the outcomes of the political choices and social struggles of the twentieth century.

Some will argue that keeping our high working hours was worth it, because it made possible all the trappings of our modern world that Keynes could never have imagined, such as smartphones, flat-screen televisions, and the Internet. Because when most people think about working shorter hours, they think that they will have to give up some of the trappings of our advanced capitalist society, things that they enjoy, like their smartphones and their televisions.

That might be true to some extent, depending on the degree of work reduction we're talking about. But reducing work time can also reduce the cost of living, because it gives us time to do things that we would otherwise have to pay someone else to do, and it reduces costs like commuting that we have to pay just in order to work. And beyond that, our current society is filled with work that doesn't add anything to human flourishing and exists only to enrich someone else's bottom line—things like the collection of student loans (which would not exist if education were free) and many big-bank positions that facilitate dangerous and destabilizing speculation.

In any case, if we were to decide to make work reduction a social priority, we could gradually reduce hours in line with increases in productivity, so that people could gradually work less and less, while enjoying the same standard of living. And while some might prefer to keep working more in order to accumulate more and more stuff, probably many others would not. Even if we can never reach the pure post-work utopia, we can certainly move closer to it. Decreasing the work week from forty hours to thirty would move us in that direction. So would something like a universal basic income, which guarantees a minimum payment to every citizen regardless of work or any of the other strings that are attached to traditional welfare plans.

TECHNOPHILIA AS A TECHNOLOGY OF DISTRACTION
Even supposing that, in the long run, the political questions and possibilities raised by automation are real, a good argument can be made that we face more significant short-term challenges. As noted above, productivity growth, which gives an indication of the number of workers actually needed to run the economy, has in fact been quite weak in recent years. Moreover, the lack of job growth after recent economic recessions can plausibly be attributed not to robots, but to failures of government policy.

That's because in the short run, the lack of jobs can be attributed not to automation, but to a lack of what is known, in the economists' jargon, as aggregate demand. In other words, the reason employers don't hire more workers is because there aren't enough people buying their products, and the reason people aren't buying their products is because they don't have enough money—either because they don't have jobs or because their wages are too low.

The solution to this situation, according to traditional Keynesian economic theories, is for the government to increase demand by a combination of monetary policy (lowering interest rates), fiscal policy (government investment in job creation, for instance through building infrastructure), and regulation (such as a higher minimum wage). And while governments did lower interest rates after the Great Recession, they did not do so in combination with sufficient investment in job creation, leading to a "jobless recovery" in which output—that is, the quantity of goods and services produced—slowly began to grow again, but employment did not return to its prerecession levels.

I do not disagree that the traditional Keynesian remedies remain important and necessary, as far as they go. And I share the worry that, in some cases, the specter of the robot future is used by the political center and right to distract attention from the short-term problems of the unemployed, in order to make it seem as though mass unemployment and underemployment are simply inevitable.

But I still think it's worth talking about what a more highly automated future could mean for all of us. That's partly because, contrary to the skeptics, I do think that the possibility for further labor-saving technology is being rapidly developed, even if it isn't yet finding its way into the economy in a way that's reflected in the productivity statistics. And it's also because even if the short-term obstacle of austerity economics and insufficient government stimulus is overcome, we still face the political question that we have faced ever since the industrial revolution: will new technologies of production lead to greater free time for all, or will we remain locked into a cycle in which productivity gains only benefit the few, while the rest of us work longer than ever?

The Specter of Climate Crisis

Thus far, I've discussed only one of the challenges that I cited at the outset, the threat posed by technology that displaces workers. But the second, the ecological crisis, is at least as significant for the future of capitalism and of the human race. The scientific consensus about climate change is clear. Human carbon emissions are warming the atmosphere, leading to hotter temperatures, extreme weather, and shortages of water and other essential resources. Differences of opinion chiefly concern how serious the effects will be, how disruptive they will be to human civilization, and how (or whether) it will be possible to adjust to those disruptions.

Many readers will no doubt be thinking that this does not exhaust the limits of debate, for there are also those who deny the existence of human-caused climate change entirely. These people certainly exist, and they are backed by very deep-pocketed corporate interests and have prominent advocates within major political parties. But it would be a mistake to take these people as proponents of a serious scientific debate. The small fringe of writers and scientists who promote denialist theories may or may not be sincere in their claims to pursue truth, but their funders must be regarded as cynics, whose actions promote a different agenda.

For as we will see in a later chapter, the key question surrounding climate change is not whether climate change is occurring, but rather who will survive the change. Even in the worst-case scenarios, scientists are not arguing that the Earth will become totally uninhabitable. What will happen—and is happening—is that struggles over space and resources will intensify as habitats degrade. In this context—and particularly in concert with the technological trends discussed above—it may be possible for a small elite to continue to pollute the planet, protecting their own comfort while condemning most of the world's population to misery. It is that agenda, not any serious engagement with climate science, that drives corporate titans in the direction of denialism.

Not all capitalists are committed to denialism, however. Some who acknowledge the magnitude of climate change nevertheless insist that that we can trust the workings of the free market to deliver solutions. But while this is not in fact totally absurd, it is highly misleading. For the enlightened eco-capitalists turn out to not really be so different from the troglodyte denialists.

Entrepreneurs, we are assured, will find new green technologies that will move us away from fossil fuel dependence without government intervention. But in many cases, these innovations involve high-tech green solutions that are only accessible to the rich. At the same time, truly global solutions are rejected, even when, as in the case of taxing carbon, they are ostensibly "market" solutions. The initiatives that excite the eco-capitalists are, instead, fanciful projects of "geoengineering" that attempt to manipulate the climate, despite the uncertain efficacy and unknown side effects of such procedures. As with the Koch brothers and their denialist ilk, the eco-capitalists are concerned primarily with preserving the prerogatives and lifestyles of the elite, even if they put a more environmentalist veneer on this agenda. We will return to all of this in Chapter 4.

I turn now to the specific purpose of this book.

Politics in Command

Why, the reader might ask, is it even necessary to write another book about automation and the postwork future? The topic has become an entire subgenre in recent years; Brynjolfsson and McAfee are just one example. Others include Ford's *Rise of the Robots* and articles from the *Atlantic*'s Derek Thompson, *Slate*'s Farhad Manjoo, and *Mother Jones*'s Kevin Drum.[20] Each insists that technology is rapidly making work obsolete, but they flail vainly at an answer to the problem of making sure that technology leads to shared prosperity rather than increasing inequality. At best, like Brynjolfsson and McAfee, they fall back on familiar liberal bromides: entrepreneurship and education will allow us all to thrive even if all of our current work is automated away.

The one thing missing from all these accounts, the thing I want to inject into this debate, is *politics*, and specifically *class struggle*. As Mike Konczal of the Roosevelt Institute has pointed out, these projections of a postwork future tend

---

20 Ford, *Rise of the Robots*; Derek Thompson, "A World Without Work," *Atlantic*, July/August 2015; Farhad Manjoo, "Will Robots Steal Your Job?," Slate.com, September 26, 2011; Drum, "Welcome Robot Overlords."

toward a hazy technocratic utopianism, a "forward projec-
tion of the Keynesian-Fordism of the past," in which
"prosperity leads to redistribution leads to leisure and public
goods."[21] Thus, while the transition may be difficult in places,
we should ultimately be content with accelerating technological development and reassure ourselves that all will be for
the best in the best of all possible worlds.

This outlook ignores the central defining features of the
society we currently live in: capitalist class and property
relations. Who benefits from automation, and who loses, is
ultimately a consequence not of the robots themselves, but
of who owns them. Hence it is impossible to understand the
unfolding of the ecological crisis and developments in automation without understanding a third crisis through which
both are mediated, the crisis of the capitalist economy. For
neither climate change nor automation can be understood
as problems (or solutions) in and of themselves. What is so
dangerous, rather, is the way they manifest themselves in
an economy dedicated to maximizing profits and growth,
and in which money and power are held in the hands of a
tiny elite.

The growing inequality of wealth and income in the world
has become an increasing focus of attention from activists,
politicians, and pundits. Occupy Wall Street struck a chord
with the slogan "we are the 99 percent," drawing attention to
the fact that almost all the gains from economic growth in

---

21   Mike Konczal, "The Hard Work of Taking Apart Post-Work
Fantasy," NextNewDeal.net, 2015.

recent decades have accrued to 1 percent or less of the population. Economist Thomas Piketty scored an improbable best seller with *Capital in the Twenty-First Century*, a massive treatise about the history of wealth and the prospect of an increasingly unequal world.[22]

The two crises I've described are fundamentally about inequality as well. They are about the distribution of scarcity and abundance, about who will pay the costs of ecological damage and who will enjoy the benefits of a highly productive, automated economy. There are ways to reckon with the human impact on the Earth's climate, and there are ways to ensure that automation brings material prosperity for all rather than impoverishment and desperation for most. But those possible futures will require a very different kind of economic system than the one that became globally dominant by the late twentieth century.

Four Futures

In his three-hour meditation on the representation of Los Angeles in movies, *Los Angeles Plays Itself*, film scholar Thom Andersen suggests that "if we can appreciate documentaries for their dramatic qualities, perhaps we can appreciate fiction films for their documentary revelations."[23] This book tries to incorporate that insight.

22   Thomas Piketty, *Capital in the Twenty-First Century*, trans. Arthur Goldhammer, Cambridge, MA: Harvard University Press, 2014.
23   Thom Andersen, *Los Angeles Plays Itself*, Thom Andersen Productions, 2003.

This is not quite a normal work of nonfiction, but it also is not fiction, nor would I put myself in the genre of "futurism." Rather, it is an attempt to use the tools of social science in combination with those of speculative fiction to explore the space of possibilities in which our future political conflicts will play out. Call it a type of "social science fiction."

One way of differentiating social science from science fiction is that the first is about describing the world that is, while the second speculates about a world that might be. But really, both are a mixture of imagination and empirical investigation, put together in different ways. Both attempt to understand empirical facts and lived experience as something that is shaped by abstract—and not directly perceptible—structural forces.

Certain types of speculative fiction are more attuned than others to the particularities of social structure and political economy. In *Star Wars*, you don't really care about the details of the galactic political economy. And when the author tries to flesh them out, as George Lucas did in his widely derided *Star Wars* prequel movies, it only gums up the story. In a world like *Star Trek*, on the other hand, these details actually matter. Even though *Star Wars* and *Star Trek* might superficially look like similar tales of space travel and swashbuckling, they are fundamentally different types of fiction. The former exists only for its characters and its mythic narrative, while the latter wants to root its characters in a richly and logically structured social world.

This is related to, but transcends, a distinction that is customarily made among science fiction fans, between "hard" and "soft" science fiction. The former is supposed to be more plausible by way of its grounding in present-day science. But this distinction reflects the biases of the genre's traditional fan base and its fetishization of the natural sciences. The more important distinction, as just mentioned, is between the stories that take their world-building seriously, and those that don't. What is called soft science fiction is sometimes just *Star Wars*–style adventure stories, but sometimes it makes much richer use of social science. Meanwhile many of the supposedly "harder" counterparts pair detailed exegeses of physics with naïve or utterly conventional understandings of social relations and human behavior. Ken MacLeod's Fall Revolution novels, which tell a tale of political upheaval and space colonization, are rooted in his understanding of Marxist political economy and his personal background in the Scottish socialist movement of the 1970s. It is that grounding, rather than any particular insight into the physics of space travel or Martian terraforming, that gives the novels their "hardness."

Speculative fiction as a tool of social analysis and critique goes back at least as far as H. G. Wells's *The Time Machine*—if not Mary Shelley's *Frankenstein*—but the field has grown particularly rich of late. In popular culture, this can be seen even in the enormous success of dystopian young adult fictions like *The Hunger Games* and *Divergent*. But while such stories are fairly transparent allegories of the class society we already live in, it is not hard to find others who have pushed the boundary further, speculating about the long-term implications of present-day trends.

The interface between the actual and the potential manifests itself most potently in the near-future fictions of those authors who place their stories just a few steps ahead of the present, like William Gibson in his early twenty-first-century series of novels (*Pattern Recognition*, *Spook Country*, *Zero History*) or Cory Doctorow in *Homeland* (and the forthcoming *Walkaway*). The significance of information technology, automation, surveillance, ecological destruction—themes that will echo throughout this book—recur in these novels.

The political implications of different imagined worlds have also begun to come to the fore. Charles Stross is both an author of social science fiction and a frequent blogger in a more social scientific mode. He has particularly criticized the popular "steampunk" subgenre. He notes that it presents a kind of idealized nineteenth century full of zeppelins and steam-powered gadgetry but glosses over the key social relations of that era: the Dickensian misery of the working class and the horrors of colonialism. But Stross, and others like Ken MacLeod and China Miéville, have used fictions about future, past, and alternative worlds to give a fuller picture of class and social conflict.

Fictional futures are, in my view, preferable to those works of "futurism" that attempt to directly predict the future, obscuring its inherent uncertainty and contingency and thereby stultifying the reader. Within the areas discussed in this book, a paradigmatic futurist would be someone like Ray Kurzweil, who confidently predicts that by 2049, computers will have achieved humanlike intelligence, with all manner of world-changing consequences.[24] Such prognostications generally end up unconvincing as prophecy and unsatisfying as fiction. Science fiction is to futurism what social theory is to conspiracy theory: an altogether richer, more honest, and more humble enterprise. Or to put it another way, it is always more interesting to read an account that derives the general from the particular (social theory) or the particular from the general (science fiction), rather than attempting to go from the general to the general (futurism) or the particular to the particular (conspiracism).

Rosa Luxemburg, the great early twentieth-century socialist theorist and organizer, popularized a slogan: "Bourgeois society stands at the crossroads, either transition to socialism or regression into barbarism."[25] That's truer today than it has ever been. In this book, I will suggest not two but four possible outcomes—two socialisms and two barbarisms, if you will. The four chapters that follow can be thought of as what the sociologist Max Weber called "ideal types": simplified, pure models of how society can be organized, designed to illuminate a few key issues that confront us today and will confront us in the future—part social science, part science fiction. Real life, of course, is always much more complicated, but the point of an ideal type is to focus on specific issues, setting others aside.

24   Ray Kurzweil, *The Singularity Is Near: When Humans Transcend Biology*, New York: Penguin, 2005.
25   Rosa Luxemburg, *The Junius Pamphlet: The Crisis in the German Social Democracy*, Marxists.org, 1915.

The aim is to develop an understanding of our present moment and map the possible futures that lie ahead in stylized form. The basic assumption is that the trend toward increasing automation will continue in all domains of the economy. Moreover, I will not make the assumption that was made by most economists in the twentieth century: that even as some jobs are eliminated by mechanization, the market will automatically generate more than enough new jobs to make up for the loss.

In the spirit of working in ideal types, I will make the strongest assumption possible: *all* need for human labor in the production process can be eliminated, and it is possible to live a life of pure leisure while machines do all the work. In fact, this isn't logically possible, if we're imagining a world where the machines serve us rather than controlling us like those in the movie *The Matrix*. We will have to do at least a little work to manage and maintain the machines.

But I assume all human labor away to avoid entangling myself in a debate that has bedeviled the Left ever since the Industrial Revolution: how a postcapitalist society would manage labor and production, in the absence of capitalist bosses with control over the means of production. This is an important (and ongoing) debate, but the issues I'm concerned with will be clearer if I can set it aside. Thus, the constant in my equation is that technical change tends toward perfect automation.

If automation is the constant, ecological crisis and class power are the variables. The ecological question is, more or less, just how bad the effects of climate change and resource depletion will end up being. In the best case scenario, the shift to renewable energy will combine with new methods of ameliorating and reversing climate change, and it will in fact be possible to use all our robot technology to provide a high standard of living for everyone. The spectrum, in other words, runs from scarcity to abundance.

The question of class power comes down to how we end up tackling the massive inequality of wealth, income, and political power in the world today. To the extent that the rich are able to maintain their power, we will live in a world where they enjoy the benefits of automated production, while the rest of us pay the costs of ecological destruction— if we can survive at all. To the extent that we can move toward a world of greater equality, then the future will be characterized by some combination of shared sacrifice and shared prosperity, depending on where we are on the other, ecological dimension.

So the model posits that we can end up in a world of either scarcity or abundance, alongside either hierarchy or equality. This makes for four possible combinations, which can be set up as a two-by-two grid.

	Abundance	Scarcity
Equality	communism	socialism
Hierarchy	rentism	exterminism

Exercises like this aren't unprecedented. A similar typology can be found in a 1999 article by Robert Costanza in *The*

Futurist.[26] There are four scenarios: *Star Trek*, Big Government, *Ecotopia*, and *Mad Max*. For Costanza, however, the two axes are "world view and policies" and "the real state of the world." Thus the four boxes are filled in according to whether human ideological predilections match reality: in the "Big Government" scenario, for example, progress is restrained by safety standards because the "technological skeptics" deny the reality of unlimited resources.

My contribution to this debate is to emphasize the significance of *capitalism* and *politics*. Both the possibility of ecological limits and the political constraints of a class society are, in this view, "material" constraints. And the interaction between them is what will determine our path forward.

The existence of capitalism as a system of class power, with a ruling elite that will try to preserve itself into any possible future, is therefore a central structuring theme of this book, a theme that I believe is absent from almost every other attempt to understand the trajectory of a highly automated postindustrial economy. Technological developments give a context for social transformations, but they never determine them directly; change is always mediated by the power struggles between organized masses of people. The question is who wins and who loses, and not, as technocratic authors like Costanza would have it, who has the "correct" view of the objective nature of the world.

---

26   Robert Costanza, "Will It Be Star Trek, Ecotopia, Big Government, or Mad Max?," *The Futurist* 33: 2, 1999, p. 2.

So for me, sketching out multiple futures is an attempt to leave a place for the political and the contingent. My intention is not to claim that one future will automatically appear through the magical working out of technical and ecological factors that appear from outside. Instead, it is to insist that where we end up will be a result of political struggle. The intersection of science fiction and politics is these days often associated with the libertarian right and its deterministic techno-utopian fantasies; I hope to reclaim the long left-wing tradition of mixing imaginative speculation with political economy.

The starting point of the entire analysis is that capitalism *is going to end*, and that, as Luxemburg said, it is either "transition to socialism or regression into barbarism."[27] So this thought experiment is an attempt to make sense of the socialisms we may reach if a resurgent Left is successful, and the barbarisms we may be consigned to if we fail.

This doesn't mean engaging in the secular eschatology that sets a firm end date on capitalism—too many socialists and apocalyptic preachers have made that mistake. It's too simplistic to think of discrete endings in any case; labels for social systems like "capitalism" and "socialism" are abstractions, and there is never a single moment when we can definitively say that one turns into the other. My view is closer to the sociologist Wolfgang Streeck:

The image I have of the end of capitalism—an end that I believe is already under way—is one of a social system in

27   Luxemburg, *The Junius Pamphlet*.

chronic disrepair, for reasons of its own and regardless of the absence of a viable alternative. While we cannot know when and how exactly capitalism will disappear and what will succeed it, what matters is that no force is on hand that could be expected to reverse the three downward trends in economic growth, social equality and financial stability and end their mutual reinforcement.[28]

The four chapters that follow are each dedicated to one of the four futures: communism, rentism, socialism, and exterminism. In addition to sketching out a plausible future, each of those four chapters emphasizes a key theme that is relevant to the world we live in now, that would assume special importance in that particular future.

The chapter on communism dwells on the way we construct meaning when life is not centered around wage labor and what kind of hierarchies and conflicts arise in a world no longer structured by the master narrative of capitalism. The depiction of rentism is largely a reflection on intellectual property and what happens when the private property form is applied to more and more of the immaterial patterns and concepts that guide our culture and economy. The story of socialism is a story about the climate crisis and our need to adapt to it, but also about the way in which some old leftist shibboleths about Nature and the Market impede us from seeing how neither the fetishization of the natural world

---

28   Wolfgang Streeck, "How Will Capitalism End?" *New Left Review* 2: 87, 2014, p. 47.

nor the hatred of the market is necessarily sufficient, or even relevant, to the attempt to construct an ecologically stable world beyond capitalism. Finally, the tale of exterminism is the story of the militarization of the world, a phenomenon that encompasses everything from endless war in the Middle East to black teenagers being shot down by police on the streets of American cities.

We are already moving rapidly away from industrial capitalism as we understood it in the twentieth century, and there is little chance that we will move back in that direction. We are moving away into an uncertain future. I hope to provide a broad context for that future, but I do not want to create any sense of certainty. I follow David Brin, who has both written science fiction and gone by the "futurist" label, when he says that he is "much more interested in exploring possibilities than likelihoods, because a great many more things might happen than actually do."[29]

The importance of assessing possibility rather than likelihood is that it puts our collective action at the center, while making confident predictions only encourages passivity. In the same essay, Brin cites George Orwell's *1984* as a "self-preventing prophecy" that helped prevent the scenario it described from coming true. In the wake of the War on Terror and former National Security Agency (NSA) analyst Edward Snowden's disclosures about NSA surveillance, one

---

29 David Brin, "The Self-Preventing Prophecy: Or How a Dose of Nightmare Can Help Tame Tomorrow's Perils," in Abbott Gleason, Jack Goldsmith, and Martha C. Nussbaum, eds., *On Nineteen Eighty-Four: Orwell and Our Future*, Princeton, NJ: Princeton University Press, 2010, p. 222.

can question just how self-preventing that particular prophecy was, but the general point stands.

If this book contributes in some small way to making the oppressive futures described self-preventing, and their egalitarian alternatives self-fulfilling, then it will have served its purpose.

1

COMMUNISM: EQUALITY
AND ABUNDANCE

Kurt Vonnegut's first novel, *Player Piano*, describes a society that seems, on the surface, like a postlabor utopia, where machines have liberated humans from toil. For Vonnegut, however, this isn't a utopia at all. He describes a future where production is almost entirely carried out by machines, overseen by a small technocratic elite. Everyone else is essentially superfluous from an economic perspective, but the society is rich enough to provide a comfortable life for all of them.

Vonnegut refers to this condition as a "second childhood" at one point, and he views it not as an achievement but as a horror. For him, and for the main protagonists in the novel, the main danger of an automated society is that it deprives life of all meaning and dignity. If most people are not engaged directly in producing the necessities of life, he seems to think, they will inevitably fall into torpor and despair.

There are certain ways in which the 1952 novel clearly dates itself. For one thing, this was the era of high industrialism in both the capitalist and communist worlds, based on the giant factory and the assembly line. And to be sure, today's economy is still reliant on this kind of massive scale production, more so than many people realize. But Vonnegut doesn't consider the possibility that production can become less centralized—and hence, less reliant on a managerial elite—without sliding back into less efficient, labor-intensive forms of production. Technologies like 3-D printing (and for that matter the personal computer) point in that direction.

And the notion that social meaning must come from "productive," waged work is deeply rooted in patriarchal notions of the male breadwinner supporting a family. There is, throughout the book, a constant conflation between work that is rewarded with social prestige—by being regarded as a "job" and remunerated with a wage—and work that is materially necessary in the sense that it reproduces society and secures the conditions of life. The women in the book continue to perform the unpaid caring and emotional labor that has always been expected of them, and Vonnegut seems not to care whether this is important or a source of meaning for them.

The protagonist of *Player Piano* is Paul Proteus, a well-regarded factory manager who becomes a disillusioned critic of the system. Late in the book, he helps draft a manifesto that calls for rolling back automation on the grounds that "men, by their nature, seemingly, cannot be happy unless engaged in enterprises that make them feel useful."[1] But

---

1   Kurt Vonnegut, *Player Piano*, New York: Charles Scribner's Sons, 1952, p. 302.

throughout the novel, Paul's wife Anita has been engaged in something apparently useful—namely, compensating for Paul's social ineptitude, and propping up his self-confidence. Reacting to Paul's failure to correctly interpret the social cues of a superior regarding a new job assignment, Anita argues that women "have insight into things that men don't have."[2] Perhaps if men could learn such insights, they too might learn to provide forms of useful labor that cannot yet be automated. But such skills are not factored into the notion of productive labor that Vonnegut associates with full humanity, or at least full manhood. This gives an indication of what is really going on here, and it is what Vonnegut has already told us: men don't want to actually *be* useful, they merely want to "feel" useful. The problem of automation turns out to be a crisis of male feelings.

Perhaps this is why so many of Vonnegut's apprehensions about automation remain intractable anxieties, afflicting both our economic conversations and our popular culture. Even when we hate our jobs, sometimes we still lean on them as sources of identity and social worth. Many cannot imagine a world beyond work as anything but one of dissipation and sloth. The 2008 animated movie *WALL-E*, for example, portrays a world where all humans have departed a ruined Earth and live lives of leisure in fully automated starships. But the sympathetic protagonist of the movie is a sentient robot, left behind on Earth to pick up trash—a worker, in other words. The humans, by

---

2 Ibid., p. 61.

contrast, are grotesque—obese and torpid parodies of consumerism.

In order to imagine a totally postscarcity world as a utopia, then, it is necessary to imagine the sources of meaning and purpose in a world where we are not defined by our paid work. First, however, let us examine how such a communist society fits into our axes of hierarchy vs. equality, scarcity vs. abundance.

Kitchens of the Future

Although he was best known as the author of *The Communist Manifesto*, Karl Marx was reluctant to say much about the content of a communist society. Sometimes, he would speak of the transitional socialist period where workers would take over and run the existing machinery of production, but this was not what he envisioned as his ultimate political objective. That objective was communism, something that transcended labor and leisure, something that went far beyond the world of work as we understand it. But to say too much about what a communist society might ultimately look like, he thought, was a foolish exercise in writing recipes "for the cook-shops of the future."[3] History was made by the movements of the masses, he believed, not by armchair theorists.

There are moments, however, where Marx allows himself to speculate in more general terms. In the third volume of

---

3   Karl Marx, "Afterword to the Second German Edition" in *Capital, Volume I*, Marxists.org, 1873.

Capital, he distinguishes between a "realm of necessity" and a "realm of freedom." In the realm of necessity we must "wrestle with Nature to satisfy [our] wants, to maintain and reproduce life" by means of physical labor in production.[4] This realm of necessity, Marx says, exists "in all social formations and under all possible modes of production," presumably including socialism.[5] What distinguishes socialism from capitalism, then, is that production is rationally planned and democratically organized, rather than operating at the whim of the capitalist or the market. For Marx, however, this level of social development was only a precondition for "that development of human energy which is an end in itself, the true realm of freedom, which, however, can blossom forth only with this realm of necessity as its basis."[6]

The reason this brief passage is important is that it provides a wholly different approach to postcapitalist politics than the one many of us have been taught. Those of us who were introduced to Marx in a classroom were likely told that he venerated labor and believed that it was only through laboring that human beings truly defined and realized themselves. And in some places he does say something like this, although this usually seems to refer to the value of purposive self-activity in general, rather than the more narrow phenomenon of doing something for someone else in return for a paycheck.

---

4   Karl Marx, "The Trinity Formula" in *Capital Volume III*, Marxists. org, 1894.

5   Ibid.

6   Ibid.

But in the passage above, Marx is saying something different: work has been, throughout human history, an unfortunate necessity. It's important to keep the lights on, and sometimes that takes work—but keeping the lights on is not what makes us human. It is merely a necessity that we can and must transcend if we are to be truly free. Freedom begins where work ends—the realm of freedom is after hours, on the weekend, on vacation, and not at work. And that remains true whether you work for a capitalist boss or a worker-owned cooperative. The space of work is still the realm of necessity and not of freedom.

Elsewhere, Marx even suggests that one day we may be able to free ourselves from the realm of necessity altogether. In *Critique of the Gotha Program*, he writes:

> In a higher phase of communist society, after the enslaving subordination of the individual to the division of labor, and therewith also the antithesis between mental and physical labor, has vanished; after labor has become not only a means of life but life's prime want; after the productive forces have also increased with the all-around development of the individual, and all the springs of co-operative wealth flow more abundantly—only then can the narrow horizon of bourgeois right be crossed in its entirety and society inscribe on its banners: From each according to his ability, to each according to his needs![7]

---

7   Karl Marx, "Part 1" in *Critique of the Gotha Programme*, Marxists.org, 1875.

Most of us are so accustomed to capitalist relations of production that it is hard to even imagine individuals who are not subordinated to "the division of labor." We're used to having bosses who devise plans and then instruct us to carry them out; what Marx is suggesting is that it is possible to erase the barriers between those who make plans for their own benefit and those who carry them out—which would of course mean erasing the distinction between those who manage the business and those who make it run.

But it also means something even more radical: erasing the distinction between what counts as a business and what counts as a collective leisure activity. Only in that situation might we find that "labor has become not only a means of life but life's prime want." In that case, work wouldn't be work at all any more, it would be what we actually choose to do with our free time. Then we could all obey the injunction to "do what you love"—not as a disingenuous apology for accepting exploitation, but as a real description of the state of existence. This is Marx as stoner philosopher: just do what you feel, man (from each according to his ability), and it'll all be cool (to each according to his needs).

Marx's critics have often turned this passage against him, portraying it as a hopelessly improbable utopia. What possible society could be so productive that humans are entirely liberated from having to perform some kind of involuntary and unpleasant kinds of labor? The last chapter suggested the possibility of widespread automation that could enact such a liberation or at least approach it—if, that is, we find a way to deal with the need to secure resources and energy without causing catastrophic ecological damage.

Recent technological developments have taken place not just in the production of commodities, but in the generation of the energy needed to operate the automatic factories and 3-D printers of the future. Hence one possible postscarcity future combines labor-saving technology with an alternative to the current energy regime, which is ultimately limited by both the physical scarcity and ecological destructiveness of fossil fuels. This is far from guaranteed, but there are hopeful indicators for our ability to stabilize the climate, find sources of clean energy, and use resources wisely. These will be discussed further in Chapter 3.

But with the scarcity problem solved, would we all just sit around in dissipation and torpor as in *WALL-E*? Not if, as Marx put it, "labor has become not only a means of life but life's prime want." Whatever activities and projects we undertook, we would participate in them because we found them inherently fulfilling, not because we needed a wage or owed our monthly hours to the cooperative. This is hardly so implausible in many areas, considering the degree to which decisions about work are already driven by nonmaterial considerations, among those who are privileged enough to have the option: millions of people choose to become teachers or social workers, or start small organic farms, even when far more lucrative careers are open to them.

The demise of wage labor may seem like a faraway dream today, but it was once the dream of the Left. The labor movement used to demand shorter hours rather than higher wages.

People expected the future to look like the cartoon *The Jetsons*, whose protagonist works two hours per week, and they actually worried about what people would do after being liberated from work. In the essay "Economic Possibilities for Our Grandchildren," John Maynard Keynes predicted that within a few generations,

> man will be faced with his real, his permanent problem—how to use his freedom from pressing economic cares, how to occupy the leisure, which science and compound interest will have won for him, to live wisely and agreeably and well.[8]

And In a discussion from 1956, the Marxist philosopher Max Horkheimer begins by casually remarking to his comrade Theodor Adorno that "nowadays we have enough by way of productive forces; it is obvious that we could supply the entire world with goods and could then attempt to abolish work as a necessity for human beings."[9]

Work and Meaning

Getting past wage labor economically also means getting past it socially, and this entails deep changes in our priorities

---

8   John Maynard Keynes, "Economic Possibilities for Our Grandchildren (1930)," *Essays in Persuasion*, Whitefish, MT: Kessinger Publishing, 2010, pp. 358–73.

9   Theodor Adorno and Max Horkheimer, *Towards a New Manifesto*, New York and London: Verso Books, 2011, pp. 30–31.

and our way of life. As in Vonnegut's day, there are those who argue that even if a fully automated future is possible, it would not be desirable. They think that the inherent meaningfulness of work is the best argument against automation. They point to studies showing that unemployment has serious negative psychological and health implications for the unemployed, as evidence of the positive value of work beyond the wage it confers.

It's important to keep in mind that when we talk about "work" in the context of a capitalist society, we can mean three different things. It can be the way we earn the money we need to survive; it can be some activity that's necessary for the continued existence of our society; and it can be some activity that we find inherently fulfilling, because it gives purpose and meaning to our lives. For some lucky few, it can be all three. But for many of us, it is simply the way we earn a wage, something we'd be happy to be free of if we could— as shown by the market for lottery tickets even among those with supposedly "good" jobs.

Consider a study by three economists at the Free University of Berlin, which suggests a more complicated reality behind claims that waged work is a necessary source of a person's dignity or meaning.[10] In a summary of their findings for a general audience, they begin by seemingly validating the consensus perspective, noting that "people adapt surprisingly well to changes in their lives," but the unhappiness produced

---

10   Clemens Hetschko, Andreas Knabe, and Ronnie Schöb, "Changing Identity: Retiring from Unemployment," *Economic Journal* 124: 575, 2014, pp. 149–66.

by unemployment is an exception: "the life satisfaction of the unemployed does not restore itself even after having been unemployed for a long time."[11]

However, the authors go on to ask *why* the unemployed are so persistently unhappy, and in doing so they clarify an ambiguity that always arises when the effects of unemployment are discussed. Is unemployment bad for people because the experience of working is good for them, or because unemployment carries a powerful social stigma? (The question leaves aside, of course, the most obvious reason for the unpleasantness of being jobless—being broke.)

To determine why unemployment is bad for people, they examine the change in self-reported life satisfaction among Germans who move from being unemployed to being retired. The authors observe that "entering retirement brings about a change in the social category, but does not change anything else in the lives of the long-term unemployed." Yet they find that the shift from being unemployed to being retired brings about immediate and dramatic increases in happiness, even when controlling for other factors, thus demonstrating "how strongly long-term unemployed people benefit from the change of their social category while retiring and the associated relief from not having to meet the social norm of being employed anymore."[12]

---

11   Clemens Hetschko, Andreas Knabe, and Ronnie Schöb, "Identity and Wellbeing: How Retiring Makes the Unemployed Happier," VoxEU. org, 2012.
12   Ibid.

The unemployed become happier, it turns out, as soon as they stop thinking of themselves as workers. This result suggests that the harm caused by unemployment has a lot to do with the way we, as a society, regard the unemployed. We treat paying work as a sure mark of a person's worth, even though this conviction has no coherent rationale.

Some who may accept this argument will still argue that the problem with transcending work is that some things simply shouldn't be automated, because to do so would be unacceptably dehumanizing or degrading to our society in some way. It is one thing, in other words, to automate a textile factory, but the prospect of robot nurses and diagnostic computers displacing medical employees fills many people with horror. Reacting to the possibility of robots providing caregiver services to the elderly, sociologist Zeynep Tufekci deems the process "inhuman."[13] But it turns out that it's mostly the adoption of machines under conditions of capitalism she objects to, the fear that that automation will only produce unemployment and misery. I wrote this book in order to argue that another way is possible.

She does, however, raise an important point. Care work like nursing is predominantly performed by women and is not coincidentally undervalued and underpaid. So perhaps the danger is less that such work will be automated, but that it *won't*, and an underpaid, feminized workforce will be all that's left of wage labor. Some parts of caregiving, the

---

13   Zeynep Tufekci, "Failing the Third Machine Age: When Robots Come for Grandma," Medium.com, 2014.

changing of bedpans and the like, are the sort of unpleasant work that seems ideally suited for automation. But many elderly people rely on a nurse for emotional connection as much as for physical maintenance.

Still, even some of the more emotionally complex aspects of care aren't immune to replacement—if people take emotional comfort from nonsentient animals, why not from robots? Often, what humans want is simply to be around other beings that we can nurture and be loved by, beings that return our affection in a lifelike way—even if they are not sentient in the way humans are. Those without human companions will thus often satisfy this desire through their relationships with their cat or dog.

But why does that connection have to come from a human servant? For those of us who didn't grow up around animals, it's not immediately obvious what the difference is between a cute dog and a cute robot. And likewise a robot nurse could be more comforting than an overworked and exasperated human one. Not surprisingly, this approach is already being developed in Japan, an aging society with deep expertise in the technologies of cuteness and robotics.

However, Tufekci's critique also touches on something more profound, which goes beyond the questions of work and automation. This is what Tufekci calls "deep emotional labor: taking care of each other." Taking care of each other, overcoming our isolation and loneliness, is at the essence of being human. But is what we want a world where we are all *paid* for that activity? Or one where we are freed from the need to work for wages so we can explore what it means to take care of ourselves and one another? My sympathies are with the second possibility and with the new possibilities and problems that might unfold in such a world.

What happens if production requires very little human labor or none at all? To see what such a society might look like, consider one of American popular culture's most well-known science fiction utopias: *Star Trek*. The economy and society of that show is premised on two basic technical elements. One is the technology of the "replicator," which is capable of materializing any object out of thin air, with only the press of a button. The other is a fuzzily described source of apparently free (or nearly free) energy, which runs the replicators as well as everything else on the show.

The *Star Trek* television shows and movies are, at one level, simply adventure stories, space operas in which our heroes gallivant around the galaxy in a metaphor of naval exploration. But beneath that facade, the future society in which the show's characters live is one beyond scarcity. We could, indeed, call it a *communist* society, in the sense that Marx used the term, a world run according to the principle "from each according to their ability, to each according to their need."

The show, especially in its second-run incarnation as *Star Trek: The Next Generation*, periodically refers to this fact and pokes fun at our lowly present world of money and commodities. In one episode, Captain Jean-Luc Picard encounters a man from the twentieth century, who has been in suspended animation for 400 years. Picard must patiently explain to this bewildered newcomer that his society "eliminated hunger, want, the need for possessions." And one of the alien species in the show, the Ferengi, are the perennial butt of jokes for their barbaric attachment to capitalism and material accumulation.

The communistic quality of the *Star Trek* universe is often obscured because the films and TV shows are centered on the military hierarchy of Starfleet, which explores the galaxy and comes into conflict with alien races. But even this seems to be largely a voluntarily chosen hierarchy, drawing those who seek a life of adventure and exploration; to the extent that we see glimpses of civilian life, it seems mostly untroubled by hierarchy or compulsion. And to the extent that the show departs from communist utopia, it is because its writers introduce the external threat of hostile alien races or scarce resources in order to produce sufficient dramatic tension. The rest of the time, the show's conflict turns on the quest to "live wisely and agreeably and well." There are many such conflicts to imagine, as we will see.

Is This My Beautiful Life?

Before saying more about what the important conflicts and categories of a communist society might be, a word about how we might get there. Hostility to automation is widespread, even among those who are drawn to its potential, because they do not see how to achieve that potential without leaving most people behind. That is, if we could go from being wage workers to being taken care of by automated production, that would be wonderful, but it seems more likely that we'll just end up unemployed and destitute, beholden to those who own the machines.

I share Marx's aversion to recipes for the kitchens of the future, so I won't attempt some kind of programmatic account of the transition to communism. I'll merely suggest some basic principles.

We should not assume that the end of capitalism necessarily involves some grand revolutionary movement that merely bides its time and builds strength, before seizing the state and the means of production at one stroke—the model of Bolshevik and other insurrectionist revolutionaries. That's not to say, however, that some kind of dramatic rupture won't ultimately be necessary; it would be naïve to think that the holders of wealth and power will relinquish it voluntarily. But since we are a long way from being able to force such a reckoning, we can think in the meantime about strategies that build the alternative to capitalism before it is completely overturned. This means giving people the ability to survive and act independently of capitalist wage labor in the here and now, while at the same time facilitating their ability to gather and organize themselves politically.

The social-democratic welfare state is often thought of as the antithesis to the revolutionary project. If twentieth-century communism was about the violent overthrow of the capitalist class, the story goes, social democracy as it developed in Western Europe and elsewhere was just about ameliorating capitalism's worst aspects, providing a minor safety net to protect people from the vicissitudes of the market. But though it can be that, the welfare state has a more radical edge as well. The effect of the welfare state, at its most universal and generous, is to *decommodify* labor—in other words, to create a situation in which it possible to survive without depending on selling your labor to anyone who will pay for it.

The decommodification of labor is a concept developed by the Swedish sociologist Gøsta Esping-Andersen in his influential 1990 treatise on the modern welfare state, *The Three Worlds of Welfare Capitalism*.[14] He proposed that one of the major axes along which different national welfare regimes varied was the degree to which they decommodified labor. The motivation for this idea is the recognition (going back to Marx) that under capitalism people's labor-power becomes a commodity, which they sell on the market in order to earn the means of supporting themselves. For most of us, our labor is in fact the only thing we have to sell, and selling it is the only way to get by.

Esping-Andersen describes the *de*commodification of labor as the situation in which you can procure your basic needs—housing, health care, or just money—without having to take a job and without having to satisfy any bureaucratic condition. To the extent that you get these things simply as a *right* of being a citizen, rather than in return for doing something, your labor has been decommodified.

---

14   Gøsta Esping-Andersen, *The Three Worlds of Welfare Capitalism*, Cambridge, UK: Polity, 1990.

So long as the society remains a capitalist one, it is never possible for all labor to be totally decommodified, because in that case nothing would compel workers to take a job working for someone else, and capital accumulation would grind to a halt. Capitalism doesn't work unless bosses can find a pool of workers who have no choice but to accept the jobs they offer. However, insofar as there are programs like unemployment protection, socialized medicine, and guaranteed income security in retirement—and insofar as eligibility for these programs is treated as a universal right—we can say that labor has been partially decommodified. On the basis of this argument, Esping-Andersen differentiates those welfare regimes that are highly decommodifying (such as the Nordic countries) from those in which workers are still much more dependent on the market (such as the United States).

And there are those who argue that certain kinds of reforms, particularly those that decommodify labor, can point in more radical directions. The French socialist André Gorz is responsible for a well-known theorization of this idea. In one of his early works from the late 1960s, *Strategy for Labor,* he attempted to do away with the tired Left debate over "reform or revolution" and replace it with a new distinction.[15] Socialists had argued endlessly, as they do to this day, about whether it was possible to use the machinery of elections and policy reforms to overcome capitalism, or whether only a violent seizure of power would do. To Gorz, this was a false debate and a distraction from the real issue:

---

15   André Gorz, *Strategy for Labor,* Boston, MA: Beacon Press, 1967.

Is it possible *from within*—that is to say, without having previously destroyed capitalism—to impose anti-capitalist solutions which will not immediately be incorporated into and subordinated to the system? This is the old question of "reform or revolution." This was (or is) a paramount question when the movement had (or has) the choice between a struggle for reforms and armed insurrection. Such is no longer the case in Western Europe; here there is no longer an alternative. The question here revolves around the possibility of "revolutionary reforms," that is to say, of reforms which advance toward a radical transformation of society. Is this possible?[16]

Gorz goes on to distinguish "reformist reforms," which subordinate themselves to the need to preserve the functioning of the existing system, from the radical alternative:

A non-reformist reform is determined not in terms of what can be, but what should be. And finally, it bases the possibility of attaining its objective on the implementation of fundamental political and economic changes. These changes can be sudden, just as they can be gradual. But in any case they assume a modification of the relations of power; they assume that the workers will take over powers or assert a force (that is to say, a non-institutionalized force) strong enough to establish, maintain, and expand those tendencies within the system which serve to weaken

---

16   Ibid., p. 6.

capitalism and to shake its joints. They assume structural reforms.[17]

One of Gorz's examples of a nonreformist reform is now commonly known as the universal basic income. This is simply the proposal to grant every person a guaranteed amount of money that they would receive absolutely unconditionally, irrespective of work or any other qualification. The grant would ideally be set high enough to allow people to live at a level of basic decency whether or not they work.

This is obviously a radical proposal, given that it subverts the typical insistence by both liberals and conservatives that social benefits be tied to work in some way or else be targeted at particular constituencies like the elderly and people with disabilities. There is an extensive debate on the practicalities of the proposal—how to pay for it, of course, but also what programs it should replace. Replacing unemployment insurance or welfare checks is one thing, but replacing health care coverage with a flat payment is more problematic, because different people have wildly different needs for health care services. But here I am more concerned with utopian speculation about the possible social effects of a universal basic income.

One criticism of the basic income is that it will not be systemically viable over the long run, as people increasingly drop out of paid labor and undermine the tax base that funds the basic income in the first place. But from another point of

17   Ibid., pp. 7–8.

view, this prospect is precisely what makes basic income a nonreformist reform. Thus one can sketch out a more programmatic kind of utopianism that uses the basic income as its point of departure. One gesture in this direction is Robert van der Veen and Philippe van Parijs's 1986 essay, "A Capitalist Road to Communism."[18]

The essay begins from the proposition that Marxism's ultimate end is not socialism but rather a communist society that abolishes both exploitation (that is, people getting paid less than the true value of their work) and alienation, much like Marx's "realm of freedom" discussed above: "productive activities need no longer be prompted by external rewards."[19]

Suppose, they say, "that it is possible to provide everyone with a universal grant sufficient to cover his or her 'fundamental needs' without this involving the economy in a downward spiral. How does the economy evolve once such a universal grant is introduced?"[20]

Their answer is that the basic income would "twist" the capitalist drive to increase productivity:

Entitlement to a substantial universal grant will simultaneously push up the wage rate for unattractive, unrewarding work (which no one is now forced to accept in order to survive) and bring down the average wage

---

18   Robert J. van der Veen and Philippe van Parijs, "A Capitalist Road to Communism," *Theory and Society* 15: 5, 1986, pp. 635–55.

19   Ibid., p. 637.

20   Ibid., p. 645.

rate for attractive, intrinsically rewarding work (because fundamental needs are covered anyway, people can now accept a high-quality job paid far below the guaranteed income level). Consequently, the capitalist logic of profit will, much more than previously, foster technical innovation and organizational change that improve the quality of work and thereby reduce the drudgery required per unit of product.[21]

If you extrapolate this trend forward, you reach a situation where all wage labor is gradually eliminated. Undesirable work is fully automated, as employers feel increasing pressure to automate because labor is no longer too cheap. The reasoning here is that, as I argued in the last chapter, one of the things holding back full automation of the economy isn't that the technical solutions are lacking, it's that wages are so low that it's cheaper to hire humans than to buy machines. But with access to a basic income, workers will be less willing to accept unpleasant and low-paying jobs, and employers will have incentive to find ways to automate those jobs.

Meanwhile, the wage for desirable work eventually falls to zero, because people are both willing to do it for free and able to do so because a basic income supplies their essential needs. As Gorz puts it in a later work, *Critique of Economic Reason*, certain activities "may be partially repatriated into the sphere of autonomous activities and reduce the demand for these

---

21   Ibid., p. 646.

things to be provided by external services, whether public or commercial."[22]

The long-run trajectory, therefore, is one in which people come to depend less and less on the basic income, because the things they want and need do not have to be purchased for money. Some things can be produced freely and automatically, as 3-D printing and digital copying technologies evolve into something like *Star Trek*'s replicator. Other things have become the product of voluntary cooperative activity rather than waged work. It therefore comes to pass that the tax base for the basic income is undermined—but rather than creating an insoluble crisis, as in the hands of basic income critics, the withering away of the money economy, and its corresponding tax base, becomes the path to utopia.

Consider, for example, a basic income that is linked to the size of GDP. We are used to a capitalist world in which the increase in material prosperity corresponds to a rise in GDP, the measured value of economic activity in money. But as wage labor comes to be replaced either by automation or voluntary activity, GDP would begin to fall, and the basic income with it. This would not lead to lowered standards of living, because the falling GDP here also denotes a decline in the *cost* of living. Just like the socialist state withers away in certain versions of traditional Marxism, the basic income withers away. As Van der Veen and Van Parijs

---

22   André Gorz, *Critique of Economic Reason*, New York and London: Verso Books, 1989, p. 169.

put it, "capitalist societies will smoothly move toward full communism."[23]

Let a Hundred Status Hierarchies Bloom

Having set the technical parameters and written some of the backstory, we can imagine that we live in a communist society. So now we return to the more human question: in a communist society, what do we do all day? The kind of communism I've described is sometimes mistakenly construed, by both its critics and its adherents, as a society in which hierarchy and conflict are wholly absent. But rather than see the abolition of the capital-wage relation as a single-shot solution to all possible social problems, it is perhaps better to think of it in the terms used by political scientist Corey Robin, as a way to "convert hysterical misery into ordinary unhappiness."[24]

For it is surely not the case that all hierarchies and conflicts, even now, can be reduced to the logic of capital. At the same time, so long as most people are dependent on wage labor, it is also impossible to completely *separate* any given conflict from that fundamental one. Rather than thinking of the capital relation as the root from which all oppression and conflict grows, perhaps a better metaphor would be that the conflict between capital and labor shapes other social

---

23   Van der Veen and Van Parijs, "A Capitalist Road to Communism," p. 646.
24   Corey Robin, "Socialism: Converting Hysterical Misery into Ordinary Unhappiness for a Hundred Years," CoreyRobin.com, 2013.

relations the way a magnetic field influences the objects around it.

In a common lesson about electromagnetic forces, students are given an exercise in which a bar magnet is placed on a table surrounded by scattered iron filings. The invisible field surrounding the magnet will draw the filings into alignment with it, until the swirling starburst shape of the field becomes visible. The capital relation is a kind of social magnet, with capital at one end and labor at the other, that tends to align all other social hierarchies with the master hierarchy based on money. Hence the hierarchy of athletic ability is translated into a hierarchy of payment for performing professionally. And yet the magnetism of capital is not so strong that it can *perfectly* align all the systems. Fame, for example, may in general be translatable into money (as when Kim Kardashian releases a smartphone game that becomes wildly successful), but the conversion is not an exact or uniform one. And while money can also buy fame, it may not always be of the sort intended, as teenager Rebecca Black discovered when her mother paid $4,000 for a music video so cringe-inducing and terrible that it became a viral media sensation.[25]

The most interesting questions about communist society pertain to the operation of status competitions of various kinds, after the organizing force of the capital relation has been removed. And once again, fiction is a helpful

---

25   Pamela Chelin, "Rebecca Black Fighting Ark Music Factory over 'Friday,'" Cnn.com, 2011.

illustration. This time, however, it is not necessary to conjure starships and aliens in order to imagine the tribulations of a communist future.

Cory Doctorow's 2003 novel *Down and Out in the Magic Kingdom* imagines a postscarcity world that is set in a recognizable extrapolation of the present day United States.[26] Just as in *Star Trek*, material scarcity has been superseded in this world, which is run according to the principle of "ad-hocracy," a sort of anarchism in which society is run by groups that form and disperse without being subject to any overarching hierarchy. But Doctorow grasps that within human societies, certain immaterial goods will always be inherently scarce: reputation, respect, esteem among one's peers. Thus, the book revolves around various characters' attempts to accumulate "Whuffie," which are virtual brownie points that represent the goodwill you have accumulated from others (think of a generalized form of Facebook upvotes or Twitter retweets). The people in the book believe that, as the main character says at one point,

> Whuffie recaptured the true essence of money: in the old days, if you were broke but respected, you wouldn't starve; contrariwise, if you were rich and hated, no sum could buy you security and peace. By measuring the thing that money really represented—your personal capital with your friends and neighbors—you more accurately gauged your success.[27]

---

26   Cory Doctorow, *Down and Out in the Magic Kingdom*, New York: Tor Books, 2003.

27   Ibid., p. 10.

Of course, that description of "the old days" isn't really a very accurate picture of the way capitalist society works, as demonstrated by the joke about the journalist who takes assignments for free from editors who promise her increased attention and prestige: she died of "exposure." Being able to endure survival independent of Whuffie or any other currency makes all the difference in the world.

The book's story mostly takes place in Disneyland, which in the postwork society is now run by volunteers. But there still needs to be some hierarchy and organization, which is determined according to Whuffie. The drama of the story turns on the various intrigues and conflicts that result. Without having to worry about survival—or death, given this book's cheery assumption that the dead can be easily resurrected from a backup—other conflicts present themselves, like whether Disneyland's hall of presidents should include a display that interfaces with your brain to give you the experience of being Abraham Lincoln. These debates are resolved not by who has the most money, but by who can acquire the highest social status.

If you spend a lot of time on social media, this might all sound more terrifying than utopian. But that's the value of Doctorow's book, in contrast to *Star Trek*: it treats a postscarcity world as one with its own hierarchies and conflicts, rather than one in which all live in perfect harmony and politics comes to a halt. Reputation, like capital, can be accumulated in an unequal and self-perpetuating way, as those who are already popular gain the ability to do things that get them more attention and make them more popular. Moreover, racism and sexism don't disappear when capitalism does; they can stratify postcapitalist societies as well. Such dynamics are readily observable today, as blogs and other social media produce popular gatekeepers; some are able to get attention and some are not, in a way that is not completely a function of who has money to spend. Organizing society according to who has the most "likes" on Facebook has certain drawbacks, to say the least, even when dislodged from its capitalist integument.

The same dynamics play out in the Wikipedia project, which provides another example of the sort of struggles that transcend the specificity of capitalism. In principle, Wikipedia bills itself as "the encyclopedia that anyone can edit," a perfectly democratic and flat institution. In practice, it is neither so structureless nor so egalitarian. Partly this is because it reinscribes the inequalities of the society around it: a disproportionately large number of editors are white men, and the content of Wikipedia reflects this. With only 13 percent female contributors according to a 2010 survey, things like feminist literature get lesser coverage than minor characters from *The Simpsons*.

So ending capitalism, and even ending patriarchy and racism, won't end the possibility for conflict. Differences of opinion, conflicts of interest, and personality clashes will exist in any conceivable world. And while Wikipedia is not run like a traditional encyclopedia or a capitalist business, it still has a hierarchy. It has a complex bureaucracy of administrators, editors, and moderators, with varying power to bypass screening procedures, block users, delete articles, move files, and other site functions.

Such structures were developed to protect against vandalism and malicious attempts to defame others or rewrite history by those with a self-interested motivation. But they have also had the effect of discouraging new editors, preventing Wikipedia from expanding or diversifying its editor base. A study in the journal *American Behavioral Scientist* found that the number of Wikipedia's editors dropped from 50,000 in 2006 to 35,000 in 2011. The authors of the study quipped that Wikipedia had become "the encyclopedia that anyone who understands the norms, socializes him or herself, dodges the impersonal wall of semi-automated rejection and still wants to voluntarily contribute his or her time and energy can edit."[28]

Bitcoins, Doges, and Whuffie

A contemporary reader of Doctorow's book may find that the concept of "Whuffie" resonates more than it used to, because of the renewed prominence of invented nonstate currencies—in particular, the distributed cryptocurrency Bitcoin. As an accounting system that maintains an artificially scarce points system that is nevertheless not tied to the traditional money and banking system, it is of some limited economic interest. But it turns out that Bitcoin, for all its

28   Aaron Halfaker et al., "The Rise and Decline of an Open Collaboration System: How Wikipedia's Reaction to Sudden Popularity Is Causing Its Decline," *American Behavioral Scientist* 57: 5, May 2013, p. 683.

media hype, may be less significant than some other alternative currencies that currently lack its pretentions.

The partisans of Bitcoin aspire for it to substitute for capitalist money. This means it must mediate exchanges of physical goods and services and be a store of value that can make claims on those goods and services. In other words, in order to convince people to take Bitcoins as payment, you have to convince them that Bitcoins are worth something and will continue to be worth something in the future.

Many Bitcoin evangelists believe that because it is not created or regulated by the state, Bitcoins are somehow a more stable store of value. This quixotic fixation—little different, in substance, from an older generation of cranks' obsession with the gold standard—has led the Bitcoin subculture to naïvely recapitulate the unregulated financial systems of the nineteenth century, with all their crises, crashes, swindles, and panics. The wild fluctuations in the currency's value belie the Bitcoiners' faith, as does the fact that several prominent Bitcoin exchanges have collapsed and made off with their clients' wealth, leaving their victims with no recourse, a consequence of the lack of standards and regulation.

The rediscovery of the need for central banking and government regulation is good for a laugh at the expense of a gaggle of libertarian young men, but it tells us little about the future. Bitcoin is not the only cryptocurrency, however, even though it has the most exchange value in traditional currencies, and has certainly been the most widely promoted. Innumerable rivals exist, based on slight variations of the Bitcoin code, going by names like Litecoin and

Quarkcoin. Many of these are opportunistic rivals driven by speculators. They are little better than traditional stock market pump-and-dump scams, in which a few promoters talk up the value of a company so that others will bid up its price, and then sell off their own holdings before the suckers realize what's happening. For the purposes of this chapter, however, the most interesting cryptocurrency is the one that is generally regarded as a silly joke: Dogecoin. In its rise and fall we can see a promising mechanism that may have been introduced prematurely into a society that was not ready for it.

Dogecoin takes its name from a viral Internet meme featuring a picture of a Shiba Inu dog surrounded by enthusiastic, ungrammatical exclamations. By the time of publication, readers of this book may not even remember it. And the same may be true of Dogecoin, which was launched at the peak of both Bitcoin and Doge's popularity in late 2013. Yet the community that arose around it tells us something important about the real significance of the entire class of alternative moneys.

Measured in terms of its value in US dollars, Dogecoin never threatened Bitcoin. But that was never relevant for the currency's core use. Within a few months of its inception, there were more daily unique transactions in Doges than Satoshis (as Bitcoins were sometimes called in homage to their mysterious inventor).[29] And that's because Dogecoin

---

29 Tom McKay, "Bitcoin vs. Dogecoin: Which One Is Really Worth More?" Mic.com, January 14, 2014.

satisfied a need for a different kind of currency, far removed from the traditional capitalist sort and in fact more similar to Whuffie.

Technically, Dogecoin and Bitcoin are nearly identical, but that's a misleading picture of Dogecoin's significance. The sociology of Dogecoin's community is very different, as is the problem to which Dogecoin provides a solution.

To understand Dogecoin, you have to understand what people mostly do with the currency. While people do sometimes buy valuable goods with it, the most common use is "tipping": the practice of transferring a small number of Dogecoins to another Internet user in appreciation of their witty or helpful contribution. This is encouraged by the fact that a single Dogecoin was only worth a tiny fraction of a cent in US currency.

Tipping in Dogecoins became particularly common on Reddit and Twitter, which developed easy-to-use platforms for executing these transfers. In this, the Dogecoin tip extends the practice of upvoting on Reddit or retweeting on Twitter— except that it converts those practices into a common currency, a form of status that's portable from site to site. Rather than attempting to replicate traditional currencies, Dogecoin is a way of bridging reputational karma across many separate domains.

During the initial flurry of interest, much of the media attention viewed Dogecoin through the prism of Bitcoin. There was an emphasis on its role as a speculative asset and a store of offline monetary value and much hand-wringing about whether it would be able to hold its exchange value in terms of traditional currency. And ultimately, that may be the death of it. At this writing, the Dogecoin community is in crisis, largely because of the hegemonic influence of a single large investor attempting to turn it into a Bitcoin-like speculative vehicle that can be cashed in for traditional money.[30]

All in all, the lesson of Dogecoin, and of the world of Internet cultures and hierarchies that it represents, is a lesson about the complexity of any utopia. Taking away money and scarcity as the master code organizing our lives doesn't make them simple or boring, because humans are far too complex for that. If anything, it makes life unimaginably more complicated. But it should still, I think, be regarded as a utopia, especially by comparison to what is described in the next chapter.

This may all seem like a disappointing sort of utopia, grasping for Whuffie and battling Wiki bureaucracies. Doctorow himself has said that Whuffie "would make a terrible currency" and that the world he created is really a very dark one, precisely because of the way reputational economies can start to replicate the magnetic master-hierarchy quality of capitalist currencies.[31]

But I would still argue that the communist society I've sketched here, though imperfect, is at least one in which conflict is no longer based on the opposition between wage workers and capitalists or on struggles over scarce resources.

---

30   Kevin Collier, "Meet Moolah, the Company That Has Dogecoin by the Collar," DailyDot.com, July 7, 2014.
31   Cory Doctorow, "Wealth Inequality Is Even Worse in Reputation Economies," LocusMag.com, March 3, 2016.

It is a world in which not everything ultimately comes down to money. A communist society would surely have hierarchies of status—as do capitalist and all societies. But in capitalism, all status hierarchies tend to be aligned, albeit imperfectly, with the master hierarchy of capital and money. The ideal of a postscarcity society is that various kinds of esteem are independent, so that the esteem in which one is held as a musician is independent of the regard one achieves as a political activist, and one can't use one kind of status to buy another. In a sense, then, it is a misnomer to refer to this as an "egalitarian" configuration; it is not, in fact, a world that lacks hierarchies but rather one of many hierarchies, no one of which is superior to any other.

2

RENTISM: HIERARCHY AND ABUNDANCE

Charles Stross's 2005 novel *Accelerando* begins in the twenty-first century, not too long from now.[1] The protagonist, Manfred Macx, finds himself facing down enforcers for the Copyright Control Association of America, a "Mafiya" that is on his tail for the unauthorized digital distribution of copyrighted material. Facing armed guards and a restraining order, he slips the noose only by a clever and convoluted set of corporate legal manipulations that he undertakes on the spot.

The notion of armed thugs apprehending people for distributing data over the Internet has only gotten less far-fetched since the novel was written. Macx's brilliant, idealistic hacker character now evokes the memory of Aaron Swartz, the activist and programmer who killed himself in 2013 at age twenty-six. Swartz was facing crippling legal fees, massive fines, and as much as thirty-five years in prison, all for the

---

1   Charles Stross, *Accelerando,* New York: Penguin Group, 2005.

crime of downloading too many articles from an academic database. Unlike Manfred Macx, he couldn't see a way out.

This chapter is centrally about intellectual property and the laws that protect it—such as the laws that Swartz was charged under. If the previous chapter was about the utopian possibility of a society of pure abundance, this chapter is about what happens when that possibility is present but stymied by ossified class structures and the state powers that defend them. As we will see, intellectual property and the rents that flow to it are the central categories of that dystopia.

Politics and Possibility

A characteristic failure of most mainstream economic discussions is their presumption that if human labor in production becomes technically unnecessary, then it will inevitably disappear. However, the system of capital accumulation and wage labor is both a technical device for efficient production and a system of power. Having power over others is, for many powerful people, its own reward. Thus, they will endeavor to maintain a system where others serve them, even if such a system is, from a purely productive standpoint, totally superfluous. This chapter therefore discusses how the current economic elite could maintain their power and wealth in an environment of total automation.

"Who owns the robots," says Harvard University labor economist Richard Freeman, "owns the world."[2] Hence the

---

2   Richard B. Freeman, "Who Owns the Robots Rules the World," WoL.IZA.org, 2015.

alternative to the communist society of our last chapter is one where the techniques to produce abundance are monopolized by a small elite. The concept of ownership, however, takes on a different texture in a highly automated world. When we talk about "owning the robots," we're not just talking about having control over a physical bundle of metal and wires. Rather, the phrase metaphorically describes control over things like computer software, algorithms, blueprints, and other kinds of information that are need to produce and reproduce the world we live in. In order to maintain control over the economy, then, the rich increasingly need to control that information, and not just physical objects.

All of this leads to the system described in this chapter, which relies heavily on the laws of intellectual property. Unlike physical property, intellectual property dictates not only rights to the possession of physical objects but also control over the copying of patterns. It can thus persist in a world where, for example, most objects can be cheaply and easily copied on 3-D printers. Those who control the most copyrights and patents become the new ruling class. But this system is no longer capitalism as we have traditionally understood it. Because it is based on the extraction of rents rather than the accumulation of capital through commodity production, I refer to it as "rentism."

The Art of Rent

I use the term "rent" in a technical sense, following in the tradition that goes back to classical economists like Ricardo and was picked up by Marx. Originally, it referred specifically to the payments to the owners of land, which were distinguished from other kinds of payments that could flow to property owners. The most important insight is that the land itself wasn't produced by anyone. The crops grown on the land, or the factory built on it, might be produced by people, but there is value in the land itself that comes as a gift of nature. Whoever can claim ownership of that land can therefore demand payment simply for controlling access to property rather than doing anything with it.

The original theory of "ground-rent" to landowners was developed in the context of a society that was still dominated by agriculture. In a modern economy, the concept of rent must be broadened and made more abstract. There are many other ways that property can generate income without any action by the owner. The owner of this type of property is not what we traditionally think of as a capitalist, but rather a "rentier," a term that first came into widespread use to describe the owners of government bonds in nineteenth-century France, who were able to live off interest payments; these people were neither workers nor bosses. In his 1893 book *Old and New Paris*, the English journalist Henry Sutherland Edwards compared the rentier to "the man retired from business."[3]

The old-fashioned rentier was generally portrayed as someone of modest wealth. This image survives today as the

---

3   Henry Sutherland Edwards, *Old and New Paris: Its History, Its People, and Its Places*, vol. 1, London: Cassell and Company, 1893.

coupon-clipping retiree surviving on a fixed income, a figure commonly invoked by those who decry low government and bank interest rates. In reality, however, income from rents is largely monopolized by a small number of rich people, as becomes clear when the full range of rent-bearing assets is examined. Rents accrue not just to land and government bonds but to distributed stock portfolios and, increasingly, to intellectual property, to which we will return.

The existence of rents and rentiers has always been something of an embarrassment to the defenders of capitalism. Defending the necessity of the boss who controls the means of production is easier, since ideologists can at least claim that they do something, whether it's organizing production or coming up with products, or merely taking economic risks. But rentiers create nothing, make nothing, do nothing; they just passively accept the rewards of ownership. Thus, there have historically been calls to tax away the rents from merely owning property, as opposed to the profits that come from doing something with it.

There is an entire intellectual tradition, originating with the nineteenth-century economist Henry George, that makes this policy central to its theories and proposals. In his 1879 book *Progress and Poverty*, George insisted that "the true remedy" to the problem of income inequality was nothing more or less than to "make land common property," thus eliminating the largest source of rents that existed in his day.[4] His contemporary followers similarly argue that since land "is not the

---

4   Henry George, *Progress and Poverty*, HenryGeorge.org, 1879.

product of human labor, but . . . is needed for all production," all rents on privately owned land should be appropriated through taxation and used for the common good.[5]

The existence of rentiers also troubled the great economist John Maynard Keynes. In a famous section of his treatise *The General Theory of Employment, Interest, and Money*, he discusses the rate of interest—that is, the return to owning capital—and argues that "interest today rewards no genuine sacrifice, any more than does the rent of land."[6] Interest, he thought, merely rewarded the owners of scarce productive resources. He hoped and called for "the euthanasia of the rentier, of the functionless investor," which he believed would be possible when society had become wealthy enough that those resources were no longer scarce.[7]

Scarcity and Property

Scarcity is central to the questions being asked in this book. Being the technocratic liberal that he was, Keynes believed that if paying interest to property owners couldn't be justified by scarcity, then it should and would disappear. From his perspective, the only reason to have a capitalist market economy in the first place was to allocate scarce goods in a circumstance where everyone couldn't simply have as much

5 Council of Georgist Organizations, "Introduction to Georgist Philosophy and Activity," CGOCouncil.org.
6 John Maynard Keynes, "Concluding Notes on the Social Philosophy Towards Which the General Theory Might Lead" in *The General Theory of Employment, Interest and Money*, Marxists.org, 1936.
7 Ibid.

as they want. If rent serves no economic purpose, then why should it exist?

But this neglects the power struggle that is at the heart of a society based on private property. From the perspective of property owners, it matters very little whether their wealth is justified for some reason of economic theory or social welfare. They simply want to keep their property. And just as important, they want that property to maintain its value.

Here something of a digression on the nature of property itself is in order. Before you can understand what makes some piece of property valuable, you have to know what makes it property in the first place. For partisans of capitalism, it is often convenient to pretend that property is some naturally occurring fact, but it is a really a social construction that must be delineated and enforced by the power of the state. And the very idea that all of the physical and social world can be divided up into discrete parts, each tagged with the name of an owner, is a part of capitalism's ideological infrastructure that had to be painstakingly constructed over many years.

This point is frequently illustrated with a discussion of early English capitalism and what's known as the "enclosure of the commons." In medieval times, land was frequently treated as a commonly held resource which local residents could freely use for purposes such as mowing for hay or grazing livestock. The "enclosure" of this land originally referred to the literal fencing off of parcels to prevent access, but it also refers to the process by which land was legally transformed from something to which the community had a right

of access into private property under the control of large
landowners, who were free to exclude others from using it.

Struggles over the commons in land continue today. The
Movement of Landless Rural Workers in Brazil, which
helped bring the leftist Lula government to power in 2003,
built its power by demanding that unused private land should
be taken away from its private owners and treated as a
common good, in keeping with the Brazilian constitution's
stipulation that "property shall fulfill a social function." And
some enterprising businessmen are already trying to
enclose land even beyond the Earth. Writing in *Dissent* in
2014, Rachel Riederer reports on Bigelow Aerospace, which
has requested government approval for "a 'zone of non-
interference' around their future lunar operations."[8] The
moon's surface may yet be enclosed: the spacefaring nations
of the world never ratified the 1979 Moon Treaty, which
would have banned ownership of any part of the lunar
surface.

For the most part, however, the total privatization of land
is mostly taken for granted today, at least in the rich countries. The debate over how to define the meaning and scope
of property continues in other ways, especially in the debate
over so-called intellectual property.

The very definition of intellectual property demonstrates
what a malleable concept "property" can be. While its
defenders tend to speak of it as though it is broadly analogous

---

8   Rachel Riederer, "Whose Moon Is It Anyway?," *Dissent* 61: 4, 2014,
p. 6.

to other kinds of property, it is actually based on a quite different principle. This irks even some conservative libertarian economists, like Michele Boldrin and David K. Levine. In their book *Against Intellectual Monopoly* and other works, they observe that intellectual property rights mean something quite different from property rights in land or physical objects.[9]

The right to intellectual property is ultimately not a right to a concrete thing but to a *pattern*. That is, it does not just protect "your right to control your copy of your idea" in the way that it protects my right to control my shoes or my house. Rather, it grants the right to tell others how to use copies of an idea that they "own." As Boldrin and Levine say,

> This is not a right ordinarily or automatically granted to the owners of other types of property. If I produce a cup of coffee, I have the right to choose whether or not to sell it to you or drink it myself. But my property right is not an automatic right both to sell you the cup of coffee and to tell you how to drink it.[10]

This form of property is by no means new. The writer's copyright has been a part of English law since 1710, and the United States Constitution explicitly delineates the government's right "to promote the Progress of Science and useful

9 Michele Boldrin and David K. Levine, *Against Intellectual Monopoly*, Cambridge, UK: Cambridge University Press, 2008.

10 Michele Boldrin and David K. Levine, "Property Rights and Intellectual Monopoly," DKLevine.com.

Arts, by securing for limited Times to Authors and Inventors the exclusive Right to their respective Writings and Discoveries." But the significance of intellectual property has increased, and it promises to continue increasing as the physical productivity of the economy grows.

In an echo of the struggle over enclosure, there are ongoing fights over the expansion of intellectual property into more and more areas. Fashion designers have historically not been able to copyright their designs in the United States, but large designers and their legislative allies are pushing bills that would allow them to sue the makers of cheap knockoff dresses and shoes. More ominous is the move to extend intellectual property protection to nature itself. In the 2013 decision *Bowman v. Monsanto Co.*, the US Supreme Court upheld the conviction of Vernon Bowman, an Indiana farmer who had been found guilty of violating patents held by the agribusiness giant Monsanto.[11] His crime was to plant seeds from a crop of soybeans that contained genetically modified "Roundup Ready" genes that made them resistant to herbicide. The decision affirmed Monsanto's ability to force farmers to buy seeds anew every year, rather than use the seeds from the previous year's crops.

In other cases as well, the property rights to physical objects are being transformed because of the immaterial, intellectual property claims associated with them. Until regulators issued a 2010 exemption, provisions of the Digital Millennium Copyright Act apparently made it illegal for

---

11   *Bowman v. Monsanto Co.*, 133 S. Ct., No. 11–796 (2013).

owners of Apple's iPhone to "jailbreak" the device in order to install new software on it. Similar litigation has revolved around the right of owners to modify the software that runs in modern cars and other vehicles. The John Deere Company, for example, has argued to government officials that it is illegal for farmers to make modifications or repairs to the software that runs their tractors. This is, they say, because nobody actually owns their tractor—they merely have "an implied license . . . to operate the vehicle." Thus does the property form mutate, so that even something as tangible as a tractor becomes not the physical property of its buyer, but merely a pattern to be licensed for a limited time.

All of this means that intellectual property is becoming an increasingly important component of the property held by the capitalist class. When we talk about the global "1 percent" and their wealth, we aren't just talking about owning land or factories or Scrooge McDuck's swimming pool of gold coins. We're talking about stocks and bonds whose value, in many cases, is backed by immaterial, intellectual forms of property.

In a 2013 report released by the European Patent Office, "[intellectual property–]rights intensive industries" were said to make up 39 percent of European Gross Domestic Product, and a whopping 90 percent of exports.[12] Similarly, the US Commerce Department estimates that intellectual property–intensive industries account for 35 percent of US

---

12 European Patent Office, "IPR-Intensive Industries: Contribution to Economic Performance and Employment in the European Union," EPO. org, September 2013.

GDP, a number that will only continue to rise.[13] This includes obviously intellectual property–dependent businesses like pharmaceuticals and entertainment as well as things like apparel manufacturing, where the value of a Nike trademark can easily eclipse that of the physical shoe it is sewn onto. Even that seemingly most material of trades, the oil business, can in some cases be viewed as "intellectual property–intensive" due to the large numbers of patents held by companies like Shell.

Nor has the significance of intellectual property been lost on the repressive apparatus of the state. In a 2010 article in *Foreign Affairs*, US Deputy Secretary of Defense William Lynn discussed the military's "cyberstrategy" explicitly in terms of the value of intellectual property to American corporations.[14] He predicted that while "the threat to intellectual property is less dramatic than the threat to critical national infrastructure, it may be the most significant cyberthreat that the United States will face over the long term" and warned that "sustained intellectual property losses could erode both the United States' military effectiveness and its competitiveness in the global economy."[15]

It's worth stopping to contemplate what Lynn is referring to when he talks about "losses" of intellectual property. Google, he reports, "disclosed that it had lost intellectual

13   Mark Doms et al., "Intellectual Property and the U.S. Economy: Industries in Focus," USPTO.gov, April 2012.
14   William J. Lynn III, "Defending a New Domain: The Pentagon's Cyberstrategy," *Foreign Affairs*, September/October 2010.
15   Ibid.

property as a result of a sophisticated operation perpetrated against its corporate infrastructure."[16] In other words, someone accessed its computer network and copied something that he or she wasn't entitled to copy. But presumably Google still had the information; it is unlikely that the hackers deleted it from the servers and that no backups had been kept. Describing this as a "loss" appropriates the same word that would be applied to physical property, but this is at best a metaphorical extension. What is really being talked about is the unauthorized copying of patterns, and the only thing being lost is potential future corporate revenue.

Obscuring this distinction is a common gambit of intellectual property maximalists, and it can have terrible human consequences. Vernon Bowman, the Indiana farmer who lost his case against Monsanto, faces $85,000 in damages. Those pursued for the unauthorized downloading of music have faced life-crippling fines, like the $220,000 charged against Mille Lacs Band of Ojibwe employee Jammie Thomas-Rasset for sharing twenty-four songs. And then of course there is Swartz, martyred by a careerist prosecutor and an out-of-control intellectual property system.

Anti–Star Trek

As we have seen in the earlier chapters, *Star Trek* provides a fable of an egalitarian, postscarcity society. But what does that look like without the egalitarianism? In other words,

---

16   Ibid.

given the material abundance made possible by the replicator, how would it be possible to maintain a system based on money, profit, and class power?

Economists like to say that capitalist market economies work optimally when they are used to allocate scarce goods. So how to maintain capitalism in a world were scarcity can be largely overcome? This requires a kind of antithesis of the *Star Trek* universe, which takes the same technical preconditions and casts them in a different set of social relations.

As noted above, intellectual property differs from other property because it grants rights not just over concrete objects but over patterns and all copies and uses of those patterns. And the entire infrastructure of Star Trek is based on patterns that are fed into the replicator and used as the basis for fabricating a physical object, just as a blueprint provides the guidelines for building a house.

This is the quality of intellectual property law that provides an economic foundation for anti–Star Trek: the ability to tell others how to use copies of an idea or pattern that you "own." So imagine that unlike Star Trek, we don't all have access to our own replicators. And that in order to get access to a replicator, you would have to buy one from a company that licenses you the right to use it. You can't get someone to give you a replicator or make one with their replicator, because that would violate their license and get them in legal trouble. What's more, every time you make something with the replicator, you also need to pay a licensing fee to whoever owns the rights to that particular thing. Captain Jean-Luc Picard customarily walks to the replicator and requests "tea, Earl

Grey, hot." But his anti–Star Trek counterpart would have to pay the company that has copyrighted the replicator pattern for hot Earl Grey tea. (Presumably some other company owns the rights to cold tea.)

Something like the anti–Star Trek world is seemingly portrayed in Warren Ellis's turn-of-the-millennium comic book series *Transmetropolitan*. The story centers around hard-boiled journalist Spider Jerusalem as he makes his way through the grimy, violent, and hedonistic world some unspecified time into the future. Spider has a "maker," which seems to be something like a replicator, although quite a bit odder and more unpredictable. And in addition to raw material, Spider must wait for a new season of "maker codes" in order to replicate new things.

The anti–Star Trek model solves the problem of how to maintain for-profit capitalist enterprise, at least on the surface. Anyone who tries to supply their needs from their replicator without paying the copyright cartels would become an outlaw, Aaron Swartz or Jammie Thomas-Rasset. But if everyone is constantly being forced to pay out money in licensing fees, then they need some way of *earning* money, and this brings up a new problem. With replicators around, there's no need for human labor in any kind of physical production. So what kind of jobs would exist in this economy? Here are a few possibilities.

There will be a need for a "creative class" of people to come up with new things to replicate, or new variations on old things, which can then be copyrighted and used as the basis for future licensing revenue. But this is never going to be a very large source of jobs, because the labor required to create a pattern that can be infinitely replicated is orders of magnitude less than the labor required in a physical production process in which the same object is made over and over again. What's more, it's very hard to make money in creative fields even now. So many people want to do this work that they will bid each others' wages down to subsistence levels. And lots of people will create and innovate on their own, without being paid for it. The capitalists of anti–Star Trek would probably find it more economical to pick through the ranks of unpaid creators, find new ideas that seem promising, and then buy out the creators and turn the idea into the firm's intellectual property.

In a world where the economy is based on intellectual property, companies will constantly be suing each other for alleged infringements of others' copyrights and patents, so there will be a need for a lot of lawyers. This will provide employment for some significant fraction of the population, but again it's hard to see this being enough to sustain an entire economy, particularly because of a theme that we saw in the introductory chapter: just about anything can, in principle, be automated. Watson, IBM's Jeopardy-playing computer program, is already automating the work of lower-level law firm staff. And it's easy to imagine big intellectual property firms coming up with procedures for mass-filing lawsuits that rely on fewer and fewer human lawyers, just as there are now systems that detect copyrighted music in online videos and send requests for removal. On the other hand, perhaps an equilibrium will arise where every individual needs to keep a lawyer on retainer, because no one can afford the cost of auto-lawyer software but they must still fight off lawsuits from firms attempting to win big damages for alleged infringement.

As time goes on, the list of possible things you can replicate will only grow, but people's money to buy licenses—and their time to enjoy the things they replicate—will not grow fast enough to keep up. Thus marketing will become more important, because the biggest threat to any given company's profits will not be the cost of labor or raw materials—they don't need much or any of those—but rather the prospect that the licenses they own will lose out in popularity to those of competitors. So there will be an unending and cut-throat competition to market one company's intellectual properties as superior to the competition's: Coke over Pepsi, Ford over Toyota, and so on. This should keep a small army employed in advertising and marketing. But once again, there is the specter of automation: advances in data mining, machine learning, and artificial intelligence may lessen the amount of human labor required even in these fields.

Finally, any society like the one I have described, which is predicated on maintaining great inequalities of wealth and power even when they have become economically superfluous, will require a large amount of labor to prevent the poor and powerless from taking a share back from the rich and powerful. The economists Samuel Bowles and Arjun Jayadev call this type of labor "Guard Labor" and define it as "the efforts of the monitors, guards, and military personnel . . . directed not toward production, but toward the enforcement of claims arising from exchanges and the pursuit or prevention of unilateral transfers of property ownership."[17] It includes private security guards, police officers, the military, prison and court officials, and weapons producers. An estimated 5.2 million guards worked in the United States in 2011.[18]

These would be the main source of employment in the world of anti–Star Trek: creators, lawyers, marketers, and guards. It seems implausible, however, that this would be sufficient—the society would probably be subject to a persistent trend toward under-employment. Especially if all the sectors except (arguably) the first would be subject to pressures toward labor-saving technological innovation. Even high-level managerial functions can be partly automated: in 2014, a Hong Kong venture capital fund called Deep Knowledge appointed an algorithm, a program called VITAL, to its board, where it receives a vote on all investments.[19]

And perhaps even "creativity" isn't such a uniquely human talent (if we reduce that word to the creation of replicator patterns). In a paper presented to a 2014 conference of the

17   Samuel Bowles and Arjun Jayadev, "Guard Labor," *Journal of Development Economics* 79: 2, 2006, p. 335.
18   Samuel Bowles and Arjun Jayadev, "One Nation Under Guard," *New York Times*, February 15, 2014.
19   Rob Wile, "A Venture Capital Firm Just Named an Algorithm to Its Board of Directors — Here's What It Actually Does." BusinessInsider.com, May 13, 2014.

Association of Computing Machinery, a group of medical researchers presented a method for automatically generating plausible hypotheses for scientists to test, using data mining techniques.[20] Such approaches could eventually be applied to other formulaic, iterative processes like the design of pop songs or smartphone games.

What's more, there is also another way for private companies to avoid employing workers for some of these tasks: turn them into activities that people will find pleasurable and will thus do for free on their own time. The computer scientist Luis von Ahn has specialized in developing such "games with a purpose": applications that present themselves to end users as enjoyable diversions but which also perform a useful computational task, what von Ahn calls "Human Computation."[21]

One of Von Ahn's early games asked users to identify objects in photos, and the data was then fed back into a database that was used for searching images, a technology later licensed by Google to improve its Image Search. Later, he founded Duolingo, a company that provides free language training exercises and makes money by inviting its users to practice their language skill translating documents for companies that have paid for this service. Perhaps this line of research could lead toward something like Orson Scott

20 Scott Spangler et al., "Automated Hypothesis Generation Based on Mining Scientific Literature," in *Proceedings of the 20th ACM SIGKDD International Conference on Knowledge Discovery and Data Mining*, New York: Association of Computing Machinery, 2014.

21 Edith Law and Luis von Ahn, *Human Computation*, San Rafael, CA: Morgan & Claypool, 2011.

Card's novel *Ender's Game*, in which children remotely fight an interstellar war through what they think are video games; indeed, the infrastructure for such a thing already exists, in the form of remote-operated drone bombers.[22] But that scenario is more appropriately revisited in Chapter 4, the chapter on exterminism.

For all these reasons, it seems that the main problem confronting the society of anti–*Star Trek* is the problem of effective demand: that is, how to ensure that people are able to earn enough money to be able to pay the licensing fees on which private profit depends. Of course, this isn't so different from the problem that confronted industrial capitalism, but it becomes more severe as human labor is increasingly squeezed out of the system, and human beings become superfluous as elements of production, even as they remain necessary as consumers.

Ultimately, even capitalist self-interest will require some redistribution of wealth downward in order to support demand. Society reaches a state in which, as the French socialist André Gorz put it in his 1999 book *Reclaiming Work: Beyond the Wage-Based Society*, "the distribution of means of payment must correspond to the volume of wealth socially produced and not to the volume of work performed."[23] Or, to translate from French Intellectual to English: you deserve a decent standard of living because you're a human being and we're a wealthy enough society to

---

22   Orson Scott Card, *Ender's Game*, New York: Tor Books, 1985.
23   André Gorz, *Reclaiming Work: Beyond the Wage-Based Society*, trans. Chris Turner, Cambridge, UK: Polity Press, 1999, p. 90.

provide it, not because of any particular work that you did to deserve it. So in theory, this is one possible long-term trajectory of a world based on intellectual property rents rather than on physical commodity production using human labor. What Gorz is talking about is something like the universal basic income, which was discussed in the last chapter. Which means that one long-run trajectory of rentism is to turn into communism.

But here the class of rentier-capitalists will confront a collective action problem. In principle, it would be possible to sustain the system by taxing the profits of profitable firms and redistributing the money back to consumers—possibly as the universal basic income, but possibly in return for performing some kind of meaningless make-work. But even if redistribution is desirable from the standpoint of the class as a whole, any individual company or rich person will be tempted to free-ride on the payments of others and will therefore resist efforts to impose a redistributive tax. Of course, the government could also simply print money to give to the working class, but the resulting inflation would just be an indirect form of redistribution and would also be resisted. Finally, there is the option of funding consumption through consumer indebtedness—but this merely delays the demand crisis rather than resolving it, as all of us know all too well.

This all sets the stage for ongoing stagnation and periodic economic crisis in the world of anti–Star Trek. And then, of course, there are the masses. Would the power of ideology be strong enough to induce people to accept the state of affairs

I've described? Or would people start to ask why the wealth of knowledge and culture was being enclosed within restrictive laws, when "another world is possible" beyond the regime of artificial scarcity?

3
SOCIALISM: EQUALITY AND SCARCITY

Kim Stanley Robinson's *California Trilogy* is a triptych of novels, each of which envisions a possible future for Robinson's home state of California.[1] The first novel, *The Wild Shore*, portrays the simple agricultural life of the survivors of a nuclear war, a tale that might fit into the next chapter on exterminism. The second, *The Gold Coast*, is a J. G. Ballardian dystopia of freeways, condos, and malls, perhaps a rentist dystopia if anything.

But the third, *Pacific Edge*, is something of an ecological postcapitalist utopia, and the one Robinson himself says he would most like to live in. It recounts the story of people living in the Los Angeles region and attempting to reconstruct its concrete jungle into something greener and cleaner. Robinson calls it an "attempt to think about what would it be like if we reconfigured the landscape, the infrastructure, the

---

1   Kim Stanley Robinson, *The Wild Shore*, New York: Tom Doherty Associates, 1984; *The Gold Coast*, New York: Tom Doherty Associates, 1988; *Pacific Edge*, New York: Tom Doherty Associates, 1990.

social systems."[2] In that, it captures the spirit of the third ideal type of society: socialism, an egalitarian society that must work together to rebuild its relationship to nature.

In *Pacific Edge*, our world of multinational capitalism has given way to something more socialist, and ecologically sensitive, but without being a total primitivist rejection of modern technology. People govern themselves on a small scale and work together to build a sustainable economy. However, our society has left behind a lot of damage to be repaired. The tensions in the narrative revolve around the need, as Robinson put it in an interview, "to restore that landscape to something decently livable."[3] That doesn't mean somehow recovering nature as it was before human intervention, but rather working out a new relationship between people and their environment; a major plot point turns on whether a wilderness area should be left totally wild or adapted to human use. In general, the struggle is over how to recognize and control the waste products of human civilization, rather than imagining that we can ever separate ourselves from nature.

Early in the book, two characters are digging up an old street so that the asphalt can be sent away for recycling. Encountering an apparently superfluous traffic signal, they have this exchange:

2   John Christensen and Kim Stanley Robinson, "Planet of the Future," BoomCalifornia.com, 2014.

3   Istvan Csicsery-Ronay and Kim Stanley Robinson, "Pacific Overture: An Interview with Kim Stanley Robinson," LAReviewofBooks.org, January 9, 2012.

The air warmed as the morning passed. They ran into a third traffic light box, and Doris scowled. "People were so wasteful."

Hank said, "Every culture is as wasteful as it can afford to be."

"Nah. It's just lousy values."

"What about the Scots?" Kevin asked. "People say they were really thrifty."

"But they were poor," Hank said. "They couldn't afford not to be thrifty. It proves my point."

Doris threw dirt into a hopper. "Thrift is a value independent of circumstances."

"You can see why they might leave stuff down here," Kevin said, tapping at the traffic boxes. "It's a bitch to tear up these streets, and with all the cars."

Doris shook her short black hair. "You're getting it backwards, Kev, just like Hank. It's the values you have that drive your actions, and not the reverse. If they had cared enough they would have cleared all this shit out of here and used it, just like us."

"I guess."[4]

My description of a communist society in Chapter 1 shows a world like the one in *Pacific Edge* but without the constraints of scarcity and ecological devastation. The way I portrayed that world implicitly agrees with Hank: they're as wasteful as they can afford to be, and the technical basis of that society

---

4   Robinson, *Pacific Edge*, pp. 5–6.

means it doesn't have to worry too much about conservation. This chapter is about what happens when you do have to figure out how to live within your means while providing everyone the best lives possible.

Capitalism and Scarcity

The political economy of capitalism has been concerned with the problem of scarcity since its inception, but never in a constant or consistent way. In particular, there has always been an understandable fear that capitalism's dynamic of endless and accelerating growth will collapse when faced with the depletion of the inputs to that growth, whether those are energy inputs like coal and oil or raw materials like wood and iron. But while scarce resources have impinged on capitalist development at various points throughout its history, this has repeatedly happened in ways that caught theorists of the system by surprise.

Writing at the turn of the eighteenth century, Thomas Malthus worried that the limits of agricultural productivity, combined with the inevitable propensity of the poor to reproduce, meant that it was impossible to achieve both population growth and increasing economic prosperity. To this day, those who claim that capitalism is ultimately constrained by the carrying capacity of the earth are popularly referred to as "Malthusians," even if the particular forms of scarcity they point to are very different than those Malthus was interested in.

Malthus's view turned out not to account for the factors that have allowed the Earth to sustain a much larger population at higher living standards than were possible 200 years ago, beginning with increases in agricultural productivity. However, the general theme of material limits to growth recurs in both mainstream and critical left-wing treatments of capitalism.

Stanley Jevons, one of the progenitors of modern mainstream economics, became preoccupied with an issue that is still central to industrial and postindustrial economies: energy scarcity. In his 1865 book *The Coal Question*, Jevons analyzed British economic growth and its dependence on tapping coal reserves.[5] He projected that within less than a century, economic growth would have to stall as coal production peaked and declined. Moreover, he saw efforts at energy conservation as inevitably doomed. Making the case for what came to be known as the "Jevons paradox," he argued that increased energy efficiency would simply lead to more energy consumption because the cheaper power would be used more.

What Jevons could not have known was that, while his assessments of coal reserves were broadly correct, the advanced capitalist economies would soon shift their energy base to petroleum. Readers today, however, may be familiar with the modern counterpart to Jevons's speculations, the theory of "peak oil." Originating with the mid-twentieth century geologist M. King Hubbert, this theory uses reasoning similar to Jevons's. Noting the approaching

---

5 Stanley Jevons, *The Coal Question: An Inquiry Concerning the Progress of the Nation and the Probable Exhaustion of Our Coal-Mines*, London: Macmillan, 1865.

peak and decline in easily accessible reserves, peak-oil theorists claim that the world is heading into a period of
inevitable economic stagnation resulting from the exhaustion of oil reserves. The theory gained credence when
Hubbert's prediction that the United States would hit peak
oil in the 1970s largely came true.[6]

Like Jevons on coal, peak oil depends on the idea that it is
impossible to transition the economy away from oil and onto
some combination of other, less limited energy sources, such
as solar, wind, hydroelectric, natural gas, and nuclear power.
But we now have an additional and more pressing impera-
tive: even if oil reserves were unlimited, we know that
burning hydrocarbons has introduced irreversible changes to
the Earth's climate, with dire consequences for human civilization. Some of the changes are irreversible and must simply
be adapted to. But it is nevertheless urgent that we reduce
carbon emissions massively, in order to head off more apocalyptic scenarios.

As Christian Parenti has argued in his many works on the
climate crisis, large-scale transformation on a very short
time scale is necessary if we want to preserve a decent and
livable world for the whole of humanity. The UN's
Intergovernmental Panel on Climate Change projects that
to avoid catastrophic global feedback loops and tipping
points, rich countries must cut their carbon emissions by as
much as 90 percent by 2050. The severity of the challenge

---

6   For an example of recent work influenced by Hubbert's theory, see
Kenneth S. Deffeyes, *Hubbert's Peak: The Impending World Oil Shortage*,
Princeton, NJ: Princeton University Press, 2008.

and the short time to act mean that, as Parenti says, "it is this society and these institutions that must cut emissions."[7] This challenge falls far short of overthrowing capitalism and yet still entails the monumental challenge of bringing down the powerful interests that profit from destructive fossil fuels.

Beyond Dystopia

The real question is not whether human civilization can survive ecological crises, but whether *all* of us can survive it together, in some reasonably egalitarian way. Although the extinction of humanity as a result of climate change is possible, it is highly unlikely. Only somewhat more plausible is the collapse of society and a return to some kind of premodern new Dark Ages. Maintaining a complex, technologically advanced society no doubt requires a large number of people. But it does not necessarily require all 7 billion of us, and the premise of this book is that the number of people required is on the decline because of the technical developments outlined in Chapter 1.

For this reason, we should not take at face value the farcical "debate" about the existence of climate change that persists in mainstream media and politics, particularly in the United States. Debating the reality of human-caused climate change is no longer relevant or productive. Those who deny climate science do not genuinely reject that

---

7   Christian Parenti, "A Radical Approach to the Climate Crisis," *Dissent*, Summer 2013.

science, but they are indifferent to its impact. They are, in other words, people who are sufficiently rich and powerful that they believe they can escape even the worst case scenarios while imposing their costs on the rest of the population, so long as our current social structure is maintained. Hence, they are properly to be considered in the next chapter, on exterminism.

Because climate change and ecological destruction are inescapable, the only relevant question is how we organize a response. The premise of this chapter is that problems of resource scarcity and ecological limitations can't be waved away easily. (In the chapter on communism, by contrast, the argument could be made that resource and ecological limitations could ultimately be transcended through better technology.) University of Utah political economist Minqi Li, for example, has written of the massive infrastructural transformations that will be needed to move the world to a renewable energy base. "The construction of power plants and other electricity facilities," he writes, "requires not only financial resources, but also workers, technicians and engineers with special skills and expertise, as well as equipment and materials that have to be produced by specialized factories."[8] This entails some kind of centralized, state-driven project that can mobilize resources and labor in a way that is beyond the capabilities of either the free market or the communist free-for-all of Chapter 1.

---

8   Minqi Li, "Capitalism, Climate Change and the Transition to Sustainability: Alternative Scenarios for the US, China and the World," *Development and Change* 40: 6, 2009, p. 1,047.

Nevertheless, it is important not to become trapped in fables of apocalypse, a nihilist resignation and a belief that nothing can be done. There has always been such an apocalyptic streak on the Left. This is somewhat understandable, given the current state of our politics: in technical terms, we can identify actions that have a hope of staving off disaster, but these seem so gigantic in scale, and the political obstacles so great, as to be practically impossible. We *could* undertake a green New Deal that would replace our carbon-based energy system with wind, solar, and other renewable sources. We *could* build high-speed trains and other mass transit to replace the gas-burning automobile as the center of our transportation system. We might even be able to remediate some of the worst impacts of the carbon emissions that are currently ongoing, through the technologies of carbon dioxide capture and sequestration.

But who is going to fund that, and how will the bill get through Congress? The prospects in the short term seem bleak. Thus, it can be perversely reassuring to think that achieving a better world is not just difficult, but actually impossible.

Anyone whose social network includes ecologically minded liberals has no doubt seen the spread of various reports of climate catastrophe, accompanied by the implicit or explicit idea that we are all doomed. Many of the findings coming from climate science are genuinely terrifying—the rapid shrinking of the West Antarctica ice sheet, for example, which is occurring far more rapidly than anyone expected even a few years ago. But even such epochal events, which are occurring almost instantaneously in geological terms, will unfold over decades or centuries. That's an eternity in terms of human society. So while it's hard to imagine human society dealing with environmental changes of this magnitude, it's no more outlandish than picturing the regimes of 1914 reckoning with the upheavals of the past century. Two world wars! Industrialized genocide! Nuclear weapons! It would probably reduce a socialist of an earlier generation to tears; a Rosa Luxemburg might conclude that humankind has succumbed to barbarism already, making any hope of socialism little more than a pipe dream.

Yet we have muddled through, for better or for worse. The bigger danger—as we will see in the next chapter—is not that we simply fall off the climate cliff together. It is that human civilization *does* adjust to the climate catastrophe, but in a way that only carves out a comfortable existence for a tiny ruling class, cocooned in their bubbles of wealth strewn around a wider world of deprivation.

Fatalism is the perfect complement to the equally inane positivity that pervades bourgeois discourse. That can come in the form of self-help positive-thinking bromides, as dissected by Barbara Ehrenreich in her book *Bright-Sided*.[9] She notes that the power of positive thinking is, all too often, promoted as a palliative, a way of resigning oneself to a negative reality rather than questioning and resisting it. *Think and Grow Rich* was the title of an early classic of the self-help genre, and its

---

9 Barbara Ehrenreich, *Bright-Sided: How Positive Thinking Is Undermining America*, New York: Metropolitan Books, 2009.

basic message has been propagated by various hucksters in a lineage that stretches all the way down to the Oprah Winfrey–promoted bestseller *The Secret*.[10] Unfortunately, positive thinking doesn't bring about utopia any more than negative thinking brings about the apocalypse.

Another version of this creed is the phony utopianism of Silicon Valley plutocrats. From Facebook to Uber, these new-school robber barons shimmer with self-satisfaction as they insist that the market will solve all our problems and deliver prosperity to all, if we would only get out of the way and stop insisting on our petty labor standards and market regulations.

The whole charade is an evasion of politics, whether undertaken in the guise of the utopian right or the nihilistic Left. The ruling class tells us that the future is inevitably bright; left-leaning curmudgeons reassure themselves that the future is inevitably gloomy. The result: the Left take meager emotional satisfaction from being right while our opponents take their payment in a more tangible form.

Loving Our Monsters

Suppose that we can meet the immediate short-term challenge and stave off catastrophic climate change. And suppose, further, that we can transform our class-stratified society into something more egalitarian, where all are able

---

10   Napoleon Hill, *Think and Grow Rich*, Meridien, CT: Ralston Society, 1938; Rhonda Byrne, *The Secret*, Australia: Atria Books, 2006.

to take advantage of the fruits of technology, and where labor in production is, if not totally unnecessary, relatively minimal. We will still be dealing with the ecological consequences of capitalism, many of which are now locked in and inevitable. And we will have to reconstruct everything, from our cities to our transportation networks to our power grids, in line with a new way of relating to the ecosystem. In order to consider what kind of social system could take up this task, it's worth stopping to characterize the relationship between humans and nature in any future postcapitalist world.

Considerations of ecology often tend toward a duality between humans—and their technologies—and nature. Talk of "conservation" or of reducing our "carbon footprints" implies that nature exists in some pristine state and that the task of humans is to withdraw from nature in order to save it. This way of thinking is ultimately a denial of humans as natural, biological beings, inseparably a part of nature—just as much so, in its way, as those forms of transhumanism that yearn to upload consciousness into computers in order to be free of the organic world altogether.

The view that nature exists in some stable, timeless equilibrium in the absence of human interference betrays a profound misunderstanding of the physical world, which is characterized by disequilibrium, disruption, and constant change. Natural history was full of overpopulation, die-off, extinction, and climate change long before humans appeared on the scene. If you view ecology as the project of preserving an unchanging nature, then you'll inevitably wind up as an apocalyptic nihilist: there is no way to preserve nature as-is or restore it to some pristine state, at least not while also preserving human societies.

In the end, nature doesn't care about us; it has neither interests nor desires; it simply exists. A postapocalyptic terrain populated by cockroaches and rats is an ecological system just the same as a bountiful and verdant world populated by every creature on Noah's ark. Who but we humans is to say that one is better than the other? Any attempt to maintain climate, or ecosystems, or species is ultimately undertaken because it serves the needs and desires of humans, either to directly sustain us or to preserve features of the natural world that increase the quality of our lives. The reason to avoid a future where we live in sealed domes surrounded by lifeless devastation is that this would be a horrible way to live. Even if some environmentalists may just want to save the whales, that too comes down to the priority they place on being able to live in a world with whales in it. As for the most extreme forms of "deep ecology," which view humanity as a plague on nature that deserves to be eradicated, these only reduce human-centered ecology to an absurdity in the attempt to escape it, as they project their own nihilism onto an uncaring world.

Kim Stanley Robinson's Mars Trilogy can be read as a critique and explication of the difference between human-centered ecology and nature worship. The books follow the first colonists on Mars, over a struggle lasting hundreds of years to terraform the planet for human habitation. In the first book (*Red Mars*), the planet is still barely touched, while by the final book (*Blue Mars*) it is covered with vegetation, rivers, and seas.[11] Those who support this process—the destruction of the original Martian environment—are known as "greens," while those who endorse keeping the planet in its original form—and hence unfit for human habitation—are "reds." Here the human task of shaping the natural world around our needs is separated from the impulse to preserve particular natural environments for their own sake.

Back here on Earth, the ecologist Eugene Stoermer and others have proposed that we live in an era that should be called the "Anthropocene," the period of geological time in which humans have had a major impact on the Earth's ecosystems. Some leftist ecologists are suspicious of this term, viewing it as a way of blaming ecological damage on humans in general rather than on capitalists in particular.[12] But it doesn't have to be that; the Anthropocene can simply be a recognition that ecology must always revolve around human concerns. The question, in other words, is not how we reduce our impact on nature, but how we can better manage and care for nature.

The French sociologist Bruno Latour has made the same observation through his reading of Mary Shelley's seminal science fiction tale, *Frankenstein*. This story is not, he

11   Kim Stanley Robinson, *Red Mars*, New York: Bantam Books, 1993; *Blue Mars*, New York: Bantam Books, 1996.
12   For example, see Andreas Malm, *Fossil Capital: The Rise of Steam Power and the Roots of Global Warming*, New York and London: Verso Books, 2016.

observes, the warning against technology and humanity's hubris that it is so often made out to be.[13] The real sin of Frankenstein (which is the name of the scientist and not the monster) was not in making his creation but in abandoning it to the wilderness rather than loving and caring for it. This, for Latour, is a parable about our relationship to technology and ecology. When the technologies that we have created end up having unforeseen and terrifying consequences— global warming, pollution, extinctions—we recoil in horror from them. Yet we cannot, nor should we, abandon nature now. We have no choice but to become ever more involved in consciously changing nature. We have no choice but to love the monster we have made, lest it turn on us and destroy us. This, says Latour, "demands more of us than simply embracing technology and innovation"; it requires a perspective that "sees the process of human development as neither liberation from Nature nor as a fall from it, but rather as a process of becoming ever-more attached to, and intimate with, a panoply of nonhuman natures."[14]

To take one small example, consider the "RoboBee" project currently being pursued at Harvard University. Their aim is to produce tiny robots that can mimic the actions of insects, in a collaboration that includes biologists, roboticists, and engineers. Given the anxieties of our time, many peoples' first thoughts will tend toward the potential use of this technology for military surveillance, a possibility that the project

---

13   Bruno Latour, "Love Your Monsters," *Break Through* 2, Winter 2012.
14   Ibid.

itself touts on its website with no apparent discomfort. But this technology could also be used to fill human-created holes in the ecosystem. By pollinating plants, for example, robotic bees might be able to mitigate some of the effects of the colony collapse disorder that has ravaged bee populations in the United States since around 2006. This is a mysterious phenomenon in which worker bees abandon their hives and leave behind the queen and young to eventually die. Addressing such ecological disorders with technical interventions will no doubt have unintended consequences, as have all our prior modifications of the environment. But as Latour observes, there seems little choice at this stage but to deepen our engagement with nature.

Ecosocialism and the State

So how to better love our monsters? The reconstruction of society along ecologically sustainable lines entails a significant role for governments and other large organizations. When we were considering communism, this could mostly be put aside, as people were left to freely associate and pursue their desires without negatively affecting others. But learning to live together on a damaged and resource-challenged planet requires solutions at a larger scale.

First of all, of course, there is the need to mitigate the current sources of climate change, the coal and oil power plants spewing carbon into the atmosphere. Fortunately, solutions do exist, if the political obstacles can be overcome. Although wind, tidal, geothermal, and tidal kinetic sources of power are useful, solar power is probably the most significant long-term alternative to fossil fuels. The sun is, of course, by far the best potential source of energy available to Earth; by covering even a tiny part of the surface with solar collectors, we could generate enormous amounts of power. Moreover, solar technology has advanced rapidly from an uneconomical novelty to a real alternative. In 1977, the price of solar photo-voltaic panels was $76.67 per watt; by 2013 it had fallen to $0.74 per watt. And one of the major obstacles to large-scale solar power, the need for new battery technology to store power when the sun isn't shining, may soon fall. In March 2016, the US government's Advanced Research Projects Agency-Energy announced a major breakthrough in this area, with the potential to transform the existing energy grid.

Even nuclear energy may play some role. But this is likely to be marginal, because of the high costs and long build times for nuclear reactors, and in any case reliance on nuclear energy should be regarded as an emergency stopgap because of its inherent risks. (The most significant breakthrough in clean energy would be sustained nuclear fusion reactors, which could generate enormous amounts of energy without the dangers and toxic byproducts of current nuclear fission technology. But while scientists can create fusion reactions in a lab, they are very far away from being able to do so in a way that generates more energy than it consumes—too far for inclusion even in a speculative work like this one, particu-larly given the short time scale of the climate crisis.)

Simply phasing out dirty energy, though, will no longer be enough. We will also have to take action to reverse some of what has already happened, by removing carbon from the air. Some environmentalists oppose such techniques of "carbon capture," believing them to be ruses to justify continued use of polluting energy sources. But a combination of clean energy along with carbon capture and sequestration is the best hope for a relatively benign transition out of the carbon energy era.

In addition to transforming the larger infrastructure, there is also the need to reconstruct our daily lives. This entails replacing our sprawling suburban metropolises with more densely packed locales, connected by public transportation. But as we reconstruct the city, we shouldn't neglect the need to remake the countryside as well. Cramming everyone into dense apartment blocks denies the need for space and greenery that in part motivates the desire for suburban living. The space outside the cities should be imagined not as an untouched wilderness, but more like Latour's description of the manmade nature of France's national parks: "a rural ecosystem complete with post offices, well-tended roads, highly subsidized cows, and handsome villages."[15] All connected to the cities, presumably, by clean high-speed rail.

The list of reconstruction needs goes on: adapting coastal areas to increased flooding, for example, a process that is already underway as Dutch engineers bring their centuries-long expertise to increasingly flood-prone locales like New York. So how to marshal this labor, if we are positing a world beyond the wage? Once again, of course, machinery

---

15   Ibid.

and automation go a long way. But insofar as humans are needed, some sort of national service could replace the wasted labor that today is funneled into the military apparatus.

The Market as Plan

Finally there is the issue of consumption. There will be a pressing need to deal with scarcity, but not scarcity of labor or goods as in standard models of capitalism. If we assume a truly perfect replicator, even agriculture can be eliminated in favor of machine-made hamburgers, indistinguishable from the real thing. Rather, it is the basic inputs to production—perhaps water or other raw materials, or just energy—that must be rationed. This requires some type of economic planning.

Planning was at the center of many of the key debates around socialism in the twentieth century. Could the state plan every detail of production for every consumer good? Should it merely control certain key industries? Could the market be used to coordinate production in a society that still deserved the name "socialist"?

Planning also appears in much science fiction that attempts to theorize a postscarcity society. Ken MacLeod's novel *The Cassini Division* takes place in a twenty-fourth century in which humanity has colonized the solar system and formed several distinct societies, one of which is known as the Solar Union; at one point the author describes their "Babbage engines churning through their Leontiev material-balance matrices."[16] The name of Wassily Leontiev, who will return in the next chapter, evokes the era of Soviet planning as portrayed in Francis Spufford's *Red Plenty*—a speculative fiction about the *past*, which fictionally dramatizes the attempts of mathematician Leonid Kantorovich to find a mathematically tractable way to run a planned economy.[17]

Kim Stanley Robinson's *2312* describes a system by which "the total annual economy of the solar system could be called out on a quantum computer in less than a second."[18] Quantum computing is a long-pursued dream of computer science, which posits that the principles of quantum mechanics can be used to build computers that are orders of magnitude faster than the ones we have today. Robinson's allusion, therefore, is to machines that could solve the incredibly complex problems of economic planning that were simply beyond the reach of Soviet-era technology. In a nod to *Red Plenty*, the economic system is referred to as the "Spuffordized Soviet cybernetic model."[19] And in yet another inside leftist joke, Robinson says the system is alternately known as the "Albert-Hahnel model." This refers to the Left economic theorists Michael Albert and Robin Hahnel, whose "participatory economics" framework attempts to devise a system of economic planning that is responsive to the needs of individuals rather than vesting planning decisions in a bureaucracy.

16   Ken MacLeod, *The Cassini Division*, New York: Tor Books, 2000, p. 62.
17   Francis Spufford, *Red Plenty*, London: Faber and Faber, 2010.
18   Kim Stanley Robinson, *2312*, New York: Hachette Book Group, 2012, p. 125.
19   Ibid.

Planning is clearly on the minds of many who want to imagine a postcapitalist future society with a workable economy. Yet all these examples are attempts to answer the old twentieth-century problem, the problem of planning *production*. Whereas if we assume the replicator, as in previous chapters, this is not really the problem. For consumer goods at least, people can produce whatever they want, for themselves. However, the resource-constrained future still faces the problem of managing *consumption*. That is, we need some way of allocating the scarce inputs that feed the replicator.

Here the universal basic income, introduced in Chapter 1, could be useful once again. In the context we are describing in this chapter, universal basic income plays a quite different function than wages in capitalism. And it will work to ration and plan out consumption through the mechanism of the market.

This might seem an odd thing to say, in a chapter titled "Socialism." And there are some socialists who see the market as inherently incompatible with a desirable postcapitalism. For them, the market is a fundamental component of what's wrong with capitalism, and is a source of atomization and alienation. Because markets use money and commodities to mediate our relations with one another, this line of argument goes, they are inherently less sociable and human than some other way of organizing our economic life, such as engaging in barter, self-sufficiently providing for our needs in a commune, or implementing a fully planned economy in which all enterprise is socialized and decisions about production and distribution are made through a political process. And certainly this criticism has some merit, particularly in a capitalist society in which market relations tend to permeate every aspect of our lives and subject even the most personal decisions to impersonal forces.

But a market, for any one particular type of thing or service, can also be considered as a technology, one with very different meanings and effects depending on the larger social structure in which it is embedded. In a society like ours, characterized by extreme concentrations of wealth and income, the market allocates social power in proportion to money—thus producing a society of "one dollar, one vote."

Consider the example of companies like the car-sharing service Uber, the errand-outsourcing website TaskRabbit, and the short-term rental market AirBnB. All represent themselves as part of the "sharing economy," in which individuals make small exchanges of goods and services under conditions of fundamental equality. The idea is that I might rent out my apartment when I'm on vacation, and hire you to drive me somewhere when you have the spare time, and that we all therefore end up with a bit more convenience and a bit more money. In that case, nobody has enough wealth and power to exploit anyone else, which would make this a good example of what the sociologist Erik Olin Wright calls "capitalism between consenting adults" who have equal power in the marketplace.[20]

---

20   Erik Olin Wright, "Transforming Capitalism through Real Utopias," *American Sociological Review* 78: 1, 2013, p. 7.

As they exist now, these companies really just demonstrate how unequal and nonconsensual our current system is. They are unequal in two different ways. There is inequality between the buyers and sellers of services in these systems: people employed through TaskRabbit can do little to challenge abusive or unreasonable demands for fear of being fired. Many AirBnB properties are run by companies that are essentially unlicensed hotel chains, not by individuals trying to let a spare room for a few days. And the companies themselves, backed by major venture capitalists, have power over buyers and sellers because they control the platforms on which the exchange occurs and can change the rules at will to maximize their profits. We see this starkly in the case of Uber, which has provoked strikes and protests from its drivers over its tendency to arbitrarily change their fares and working conditions.

But if we posit a world in which everyone is allocated the same basic income and nobody has control over vast pools of wealth, this objection disappears. Think of the basic income as the ration card that gives you access to your share of all that is scarce in the world. Rather than allocate specific amounts of each scarce resource, the pricing mechanism of the market is used to protect against overuse.

To illustrate what this means, consider a mundane example: parking. In American cities, street parking has traditionally been free in most areas or available at a small fixed price. This is a dramatic underpricing, in the sense that it leads people to overconsume the limited resource of parking spaces, leading to a shortage of free spaces and many cars cruising around looking for spaces. In some areas of New York, most of the traffic on the streets is people looking for parking, wasting their time while creating pollution and congestion.

As an alternative, some cities are experimenting with various schemes for pricing street parking, often under the influence of UCLA parking theorist Donald Shoup.[21] One of Shoup's key themes is that urban governments should avoid under-pricing street parking, because to do so leads to Soviet-style shortages as described above, along with tedious rationing rules such as two-hour limits and the like.

Under the influence of this theory, the city of Los Angeles decided to implement a wireless smart-metering system called LA Express Park. Sensors are installed in the pavement below each space, and they detect the presence of cars in a given area. The computerized system then automatically adjusts the price of parking depending on how many spaces are filled. When spaces are in high demand, the price can rise as high as $6 per hour, and when many spaces are available they can be as cheap as 50 cents.

The LA Express Park scheme has been widely discussed and promoted as applying the "free market" to parking. This naturally grates on those of the Left who equate the market with capitalism and with inequality. But in this case talk of "markets" is more than just an ideological subterfuge to further enrich the powerful; it gives some hints at the

---

21   Donald Shoup, *The High Cost of Free Parking*, Washington, DC: APA Planners Press, 2005.

potential of markets as limited technologies separable from capitalism.

Marxists have commonly made two objections to capitalist markets. The first is narrowly economic: under the "anarchy" of capitalist competition, the pursuit of private profit leads to unjust and irrational results. Luxury goods are produced while the poor starve, inventories pile up that no one can afford to buy, factories lie idle while thousands are looking for work, the environment is despoiled, and so on. In Leon Trotsky's *Transitional Program*, in which he laid out a short term reformist program for his communist followers, there are repeated references to this kind of market anarchy, which will inevitably be superseded by a superior form of rational, conscious, worker-controlled planning. Indeed, says Trotsky, "The necessity of 'controlling' economy, of placing state 'guidance' over industry and of 'planning' is today recognized—at least in words—by almost all current bourgeois and petty bourgeois tendencies, from fascist to Social Democratic."[22]

Yet Trotsky himself was adamant that market mechanisms had to be a part of planning the economy. In his 1932 critique *The Soviet Economy in Danger*, he writes:

> The innumerable living participants in the economy, state and private, collective and individual, must serve notice of their needs and of their relative strength not only through

---

22 Leon Trotsky, "'Business Secrets' and Workers' Control of Industry" in *The Transitional Program*, Marxists.org, 1938.

the statistical determinations of plan commissions but by the
direct pressure of supply and demand. The plan is checked
and, to a considerable degree, realized through the market.[23]

Seen from this perspective, the Los Angeles system is not a
capitalist "free market" deregulation. The city is not turning
parking over to private companies to compete for customers.
The LA Express Park experiment is in fact an exemplary case
of central planning. The city begins by decreeing a production target, which in this case is maintaining one empty
parking space on each street. The complex system of sensors
and pricing algorithms is then used to create price signals that
will meet the target. In a fundamental way, the capitalist
market's causal arrow has been reversed: rather than market
price fluctuations leading to an unpredictable level of production, it is the production target that comes first, and the prices
are dictated by the quota.

There is another argument against markets. That they are
not merely anarchic and inefficient, but also induce ideological mystifications that perpetuate capitalism and exploitation.
The Marxist political scientist Bertell Ollman has often
argued this. "A major virtue of centrally planned societies,"
he says, is that "it is easy to see who is responsible for what
goes wrong."[24] This is a precondition for democratic

---

23   Leon Trotsky, "Conditions and Methods of Planned Economy" in
Soviet Economy in Danger: The Expulsion of Zinoviev, Marxists.org, 1932.
    24   Bertell Ollman, "Market Mystification in Capitalist and Market
Socialist Societies," in Bertell Ollman and David Schweickart, eds., *Market
Socialism: The Debate Among Socialists,* London: Routledge, 1998, p. 81.

accountability, because "only a critique of market mystification will enable us to put the blame where it belongs, which is to say—on the capitalist market as such and the class that rules over it."[25]

But this critique too fails. Despite the presence of price signals, and a market, it is no mystery who is responsible for the new regime of fluctuating meter prices: the city of Los Angeles, urged on by its adviser Donald Shoup. Indeed, it is the very visibility of the planners that makes projects like this controversial among those who take their right to free parking for granted and who oppose policies like congestion pricing that would mitigate traffic by charging drivers for entering busy areas. This is also part of what makes climate policies such as a carbon tax vulnerable to right-wing attack: whatever its "market-based" costume, everyone knows that the policy begins with government lawmakers and bureaucrats.

The real failing of LA Express Park and all systems like it is that they exist within a dramatically unequal capitalist society. In such a society, $6 for a parking space means less to a rich person than to a poor one, and so the system is inherently unequal. The answer is not to attack the system of market planning, but to overthrow that underlying inequality. Ultimately, this means overcoming the capitalist system of resource distribution and approaching a world in which control of wealth is equalized—that is, where "the distribution of the means of payment" (to use Gorz's phrase cited in Chapter 2) is essentially equal.

---

25   Ibid.

But short of that, there are ways to turn some of the predatory "sharing economy" businesses into something a bit more egalitarian. Economics writer Mike Konczal, for instance, has suggested a plan to "socialize Uber."[26] He notes that since the company's workers already own most of the capital—their cars—it would be relatively easy for a worker cooperative to set up an online platform that works like the Uber app but is controlled by the workers themselves rather than a handful of Silicon Valley capitalists.

If we can tackle the inequalities that make our current market societies so brutal, we might have a chance of deploying market mechanisms to organize consumption in an ecologically limited world, allowing all of us to come through capitalism and climate change as equals—"alive in the sunshine," as the eco-socialist and *Jacobin* magazine editor Alyssa Battistoni says in a reference to Virginia Woolf.[27]

Socialism is a world of limits, but that doesn't mean it can't also be a world of freedom. As discussed in Chapter 1, communism has limits as well, but they are entirely internal to human social relations. Here, limits are also imposed by the physical environment in which we live. We can still reduce labor to a minimum, even if consumption must be bounded. And what work of ecological reconstruction is necessary can be shared out fairly rather than dictated by those with access to wealth. It may sometimes be drudgery: we started this chapter, after all, with a story of people ripping

26 Mike Konczal, "Socialize Uber: It's Easier than You Think," *The Nation*, December 10, 2014.
27 Alyssa Battistoni, "Alive in the Sunshine," *Jacobin* 13, Winter 2014.

up asphalt for recycling, and having ripped up asphalt myself, I can't really recommend it. In other cases, though, the work we do may be something that people find fulfilling and exciting. Whether it's designing robo-bees or parking algorithms, socialist ecology is full of compelling challenges, a bit of communism in the eco-socialist future.

In other words, the socialist future can be as mundane as spending one's replicator rations and reporting for duty in the Ecological Reconstruction Corps. Or it can be as grand as terraforming our own planet, reconstructing it into something that can continue to support us and at least some of the other living creatures that currently exist—in other words, making an entirely new nature and ensuring that we still have a place in it. This world may not have the giddy and improvisational feel of the communist future, but it could still be a good place to live for everyone—which is a lot more than can be said for the final future we will examine.

4
EXTERMINISM: HIERARCHY AND SCARCITY

Neill Blomkamp's 2013 movie *Elysium* portrays a dystopian Earth in the year 2154. A small elite—the 1 percent, if you will—has decamped for a space station called Elysium. There, they enjoy lives of comfort and leisure, lives that are apparently eternal due their access to miraculous "Med-Bay" technology. Back on Earth, meanwhile, the rest of humanity lives on a crowded, polluted planet, governed by a robotic police force. The plot centers around Max (Matt Damon), one of the Earth-bound rabble who has been poisoned by radiation, as he attempts to penetrate the sanctum of Elysium and access its medical wonders.

The political economy of Elysium is somewhat difficult to extract from the film, but some suggestive themes emerge. Most important is that the rich on Elysium do not appear to be economically dependent on Earth in any significant way. We do see a factory, where Max works in the beginning of the movie and which is run by one of the Elysium elite. But the purpose of that factory seems to be merely the production of weapons and robots, whose purpose in turn is to control the population of Earth. For the most part, the residents of Earth appear less like a proletariat than like inmates of a concentration camp, where populations are warehoused rather than exploited for their labor. The political economy of *Elysium* therefore differs from that of, for example, *The Hunger Games*, in which the posh lifestyles in the capital city of Panem are sustained by the surrounding "districts" where the poor produce essential commodities.

The ending of *Elysium* suggests that perhaps the life-styles of the rich can be generalized to everyone, with luxury and immortality for all. This is by no means unambiguous, however. In a previous chapter, I suggested that if such a postscarcity society were to arise in the context of class hierarchy, it would be more likely to take the form of a rentier economy centered on intellectual property. *Elysium* looks like something different: the fourth permutation of our axes of hierarchy-equality and scarcity-abundance—that is, a world where scarcity cannot be totally overcome for all but can be overcome for a small elite.

Communism for the Few

Ironically, the life enjoyed within Elysium's bubble appears not too different from the Communist scenario sketched out several chapters earlier. The difference, of course, is that it is communism for the few. And indeed, we can already see tendencies in this direction in our contemporary economy. As Charles Stross has noted, the very richest inhabit a world in which most goods are, in effect, free. That is, their wealth is so great relative to the cost of food, housing, travel, and other amenities that they rarely have to consider the cost of anything. Whatever they want, they can have.

For the very rich, then, the world system already resembles the communism described earlier. The difference, of course, is that their postscarcity condition is made possible not just by machines but by the labor of the global working class. But an optimistic view of future developments—the future I have described as communism—is that we will eventually come to a state in which we are all, in some sense, the 1 percent. As William Gibson famously remarked, "the future is already here; it's just unevenly distributed."[1]

But what if resources and energy are simply too scarce to allow everyone to enjoy the material standard of living that the rich enjoy today? What if we arrive in a future that no longer requires the mass proletariat's labor in production but is unable to provide everyone with an arbitrarily high standard of consumption? If we arrive in that world as an egalitarian society, our system will resemble the socialist regime of shared conservation described in the previous section. But if, instead, we remain a society polarized between a privileged elite and a downtrodden mass, then the

---

1   William Gibson, "The Science of Science Fiction," *Talk of the Nation*, Washington, DC: National Public Radio, November 30, 1999.

most plausible trajectory leads to something much darker. The rich will sit secure in the knowledge that their replicators and robots can provide for their every need. What of the rest of us?

The great danger posed by the automation of production, in the context of a world of hierarchy and scarce resources, is that it makes the great mass of people superfluous from the standpoint of the ruling elite. This is in contrast to capitalism, where the antagonism between capital and labor was characterized by both a clash of interests and a relationship of mutual dependence: the workers depend on capitalists as long as they don't control the means of production themselves, while the capitalists need workers to run their factories and shops.

It was that interdependence, in fact, that gave hope and confidence to many socialist movements of the past. The bosses may hate us, the thinking went, but they need us, and that gives us power and leverage over them. In the old labor and socialist standard "Solidarity Forever," the victory of the workers is inevitable because "they have taken untold millions that they never toiled to earn, but without our brain and muscle not a single wheel can turn." With the rise of the robots, the second line ceases to hold.

The existence of an impoverished, economically superfluous rabble poses a great danger to the ruling class, which will naturally fear imminent expropriation; confronted with this threat, several courses of action present themselves. The masses can be bought off with some degree of redistribution of resources, as the rich share out their wealth in the form of social welfare programs, at least if resource constraints aren't too binding. But in addition to potentially reintroducing scarcity into the lives of the rich, this solution is liable to lead to an ever-rising tide of demands on the part of the masses, thus raising the specter of expropriation once again.

This is essentially what happened at the high tide of the welfare state, in the aftermath of the Great Depression and World War II. For a while, robust social benefits and strong labor unions coincided with high profits and rapid growth, and so labor and capital enjoyed an uneasy peace. But that very prosperity led to a situation where workers were empowered to demand more and more power over the conditions of work, and so the bosses began to fear that both profits and control over the workplace were slipping out of their hands. In a capitalist society, this is an avoidable tension: the boss needs the worker but is also terrified of his or her potential power.

So what happens if the masses are dangerous but are no longer a working class, and hence of no value to the rulers? Someone will eventually get the idea that it would be better to get rid of them.

The Extermination Endgame

In 1980, the Marxist historian E. P. Thompson wrote an essay reflecting on the Cold War and the ever-present threat of nuclear annihilation, called "Notes on Exterminism, the

Last Stage of Civilization."[2] In it, he contemplated the increasing turn of both the capitalist and communist economies toward the technologies of militarism and war. It was, he thought, inadequate to understand the arms race and the military buildup as merely tools to defend the larger political economies of the contending sides, be that the planned economy of the USSR or the capitalist market of the United States. The military-industrial complex was taking up a larger and larger part of the economy in the rich capitalist countries, and the Soviets were likewise increasingly preoccupied with building up arms.

Thompson proposed that we needed a new category to understand this social formation. He quotes Marx's famous line from *The Poverty of Philosophy*: "the hand-mill gives you society with the feudal lord; the steam-mill, society with the industrial capitalist."[3] That is, as the central economic relations of a society change, all the social relations in that society tend to change with them. Confronting the logic of military industrialism, Thompson asks, "what are we given by those Satanic mills which are now at work, grinding out the means of human extermination?" His answer was that the category we needed was "exterminism." This term covers "these characteristics of a society—expressed, in differing degrees, within its economy, its polity, and its ideology—which thrust it in a direction whose outcome must be the extermination of multitudes."[4]

---

2   E. P. Thompson, "Notes on Exterminism: The Last Stage of Civilisation, Exterminism and the Cold War," *New Left Review* 1: 121, 1980.
3   Karl Marx, *The Poverty of Philosophy*, Marxists.org, 1847.
4   Thompson, "Notes on Extremism," p. 5.

The specific configuration Thompson discussed has largely disappeared—there is no longer a Cold War or a USSR. Despite the best efforts of militarist neoconservatives and others to nostalgically recreate great power conflicts with Russia or China, these hardly compare to the shadow of nuclear terror that hung over Thompson's head. And so I have repurposed his word to describe another order, the final of my four hypothetical societies. Yet what I will describe is nevertheless another kind of society that is "thrust . . . in a direction whose outcome must be the extermination of multitudes."

We still live in heavily militarized world, where the military budget takes up almost as large a percentage of the US economy as it did when Thompson wrote his essay. But the conflicts that define the era of the so-called "War on Terror" are asymmetrical ones, pitting technologically advanced militaries against weak states or stateless insurgents. The lessons learned in these theaters come home, leading to the militarization of domestic policing as well.

A world where the ruling class no longer depends on the exploitation of working class labor is a world where the poor are merely a danger and an inconvenience. Policing and repressing them ultimately seem more trouble than can be justified. This is where the thrust toward "the extermination of multitudes" originates. Its ultimate endpoint is literally the extermination of the poor, so that the rabble can finally be brushed aside once and for all, leaving the rich to live in peace and quiet in their Elysium.

In a 1983 article, the Nobel Prize–winning economist Wassily Leontief anticipated the problem of mass unemployment that has been contemplated throughout this book. In what he calls, with some understatement, a "somewhat shocking but essentially appropriate analogy," he compares workers to horses.

> One might say that the process by which progressive introduction of new computerized, automated, and robotized equipment can be expected to reduce the role of labor is similar to the process by which the introduction of tractors and other machinery first reduced and then completely eliminated horses and other draft animals in agriculture.[5]

As he then notes, this led most people to the conclusion that "from the human point of view, keeping all these idle horses . . . would make little sense." As a result, the US horse population fell from 21.5 million in 1900 to 3 million in 1960.[6] Leontief goes on to express, with the cheery confidence of a mid-century technocrat, his confidence that since people are not horses, we will surely find ways to support all of society's members. Echoing Gorz and other critics of wage labor, he argues that "sooner or later . . . it will have to be admitted that the demand for 'employment' is in the first instance a demand for 'livelihood,' meaning income."[7] However, given

---

5   Wassily Leontief, "Technological Advance, Economic Growth, and the Distribution of Income," *Population and Development Review* 9: 3, 1983, p. 405.

6   M. Eugene Ensminger, *Horses and Horsemanship*, 5th ed., Shawnee Mission, KS: Interstate Publishers, 1977.

7   Leontief, "Technological Advance," p. 409.

the contemptuous and cruel attitudes of today's ruling class, we can in no way take that for granted.

Fortunately, even the rich have developed norms of morality that make it difficult to reach for this Final Solution as a first resort. Their initial step is simply to hide from the poor, much like the characters in *Elysium*. But all around us, we can see the gradual drift away from just corralling and controlling "excess" populations, into justifications for permanently eliminating them.

Enclave Societies and Social Control

The sociologist Bryan Turner has argued that we live in an "enclave society."[8] Despite the myth of increasing mobility under globalization, we in fact inhabit an order in which "governments and other agencies seek to regulate spaces and, where necessary, to immobilize flows of people, goods and services" by means of "enclosure, bureaucratic barriers, legal exclusions and registrations."[9]

Of course, it is the movements of the masses whose movements are restricted, while the elite remains cosmopolitan and mobile. Some of the examples Turner adduces are relatively trivial, like frequent-flyer lounges and private rooms in public hospitals. Others are more serious, like gated communities (or, in the more extreme case, private islands) for the rich, and ghettos for the poor—where police are responsible

8   Bryan S. Turner, "The Enclave Society: Towards a Sociology of Immobility," *European Journal of Social Theory* 10: 2, 2007.
9   Ibid., p. 290.

for keeping poor people out of the "wrong" neighborhoods. Biological quarantines and immigration restrictions take the enclave concept to the level of the nation-state. In all cases, the prison looms as the ultimate dystopian enclave for those who do not comply, whether it is the federal penitentiary or the detention camp at Guantanamo Bay. Gated communities, private islands, ghettos, prisons, terrorism paranoia, biological quarantines—these amount to an inverted global gulag, where the rich live in tiny islands of wealth strewn around an ocean of misery.

In *Tropic of Chaos*, Christian Parenti shows how this order is created in the world's crisis regions, as climate change brings about what he calls the "catastrophic convergence" of ecological change, economic inequality, and state failure.[10] In the wake of colonialism and neoliberalism, the rich countries, along with the elites of the poorer ones, have facilitated a disintegration into anarchic violence, as various tribal and political factions fight over the diminishing bounty of damaged ecosystems. Faced with this bleak reality, many of the rich—which, in global terms, includes many workers in the rich countries as well—have resigned themselves to barricading themselves into their fortresses, to be protected by unmanned drones and private military contractors. Guard labor, a feature of the rentist society, reappears in an even more malevolent form, as a lucky few are employed as enforcers and protectors for the rich.

10   Christian Parenti, *Tropic of Chaos: Climate Change and the New Geography of Violence*, New York: Nation Books, 2011.

But the construction of enclaves is not limited to the poorest places. Across the world, the rich are demonstrating their desire to escape from the rest of us. A 2013 article in *Forbes* magazine reports on the mania, among the rich, for ever-more-elaborate home security.[11] An executive for one security company boasts that his Los Angeles house has security "similar to that of the White House." Others market infrared sensors, facial recognition technologies, and defensive systems that spray noxious smoke or pepper spray. All this for people who, although rich, are largely anonymous and hardly prominent targets for would-be attackers. Paranoid though they may seem, large numbers of the economic elite appear to regard themselves as a set-upon minority, at war with the rest of society.

Silicon Valley is a hotbed of such sentiments, plutocrats talking openly about "secession." In one widely disseminated speech, Balaji Srinivasan, the cofounder of a San Francisco genetics company, told an audience of start-up entrepreneurs that "we need to build opt-in society, outside the US, run by technology."[12] For now, that reflects hubris and ignorance of the myriad ways someone like him is supported by the workers who make his life possible. But it demonstrates the impulse to wall off the rich from what are deemed to be surplus populations.

Other trends are less dramatic than decamping to an opt-in society, but nevertheless disturbing. Around the United

---

11   Morgan Brennan, "Billionaire Bunkers: Beyond the Panic Room, Home Security Goes Sci-Fi," Forbes.com, December 16, 2013.

12   Anand Giridharadas, "Silicon Valley Roused by Secession Call," *New York Times*, October 29, 2013.

States, residents of wealthier neighborhoods are beginning to hire private security to defend themselves from the perceived threat of their neighbors. In Oakland, small groups of neighbors band together to hire their own guards, and one neighborhood even took the initiative to raise $90,000 through a crowdfunding campaign.[13] Thus do the ranks of guard laborers swell.

And there are already those who would build an entire city to hide from the masses. Off the coast of Lagos, Nigeria, a group of Lebanese developers are building a private city, Eko Atlantic, intended to house 250,000. It is to be "a sustainable city, clean and energy efficient with minimal carbon emissions."[14] It is also going to be a place where the elite can escape from the millions of nearby Nigerians who live on less than a dollar a day and scrounge in the informal economy. Another island, the island of Manhattan, is also gradually being turned into an enclave of the global rich: in 2014, over half of Manhattan real estate sales worth $5 million or more were to foreigners or anonymous buyers behind shell companies (most of whom are believed to be non-American).[15] These purchases serve the dual purpose of laundering money and hiding it from prying governments, as well as providing a landing place in case of unrest in their home countries.

---

13 Puck Lo, "In Gentrifying Neighborhoods, Residents Say Private Patrols Keep Them Safe," Al Jazeera America, May 30, 2014.

14 Martin Lukacs, "New, Privatized African City Heralds Climate Apartheid," *Guardian*, January 21, 2014.

15 Louise Story and Stephanie Saul, "Stream of Foreign Wealth Flows to Elite New York Real Estate." *New York Times*, February 7, 2015.

At the intersection of paranoia and tasteless consumption, there's Vivos, whose website promises "the ultimate life assurance solution for high net worth families." The company is building an eighty-apartment, radiation-proof megabunker, carved into a mountain in Germany. These aren't your ordinary bomb-shelters, but rather luxury apartments featuring all the leather and stainless steel trappings of the *nouveau riche*. Company founder Robert Vicino described the complex to the *Vice* website as comparable to "an underground yacht." For a mere 2.5 million Euros and up, you too can wait out the apocalypse in style. And Vivos is only one example of what *Forbes* magazine called the "Billionaires' Bunkers" industry.[16]

From Enclave to Genocide

Today, we laugh at out-of-touch billionaires like venture capitalist Tom Perkins, who in 2014 compared criticism of the rich to Kristallnacht, the attacks on Jews in Nazi Germany in 1938.[17] Or Cartier jewelry executive Johann Rupert, who told a 2015 *Financial Times* conference that the prospect of an insurgency among the poor is "what keeps me awake at night."[18] But while such views are repugnant, they are not without logic. In a world of hyperinequality and mass

16   Morgan Brennan, "Billionaires' Bunkers."
17   Tom Perkins, "Progressive Kristallnacht Coming?" *Wall Street Journal*, January 24, 2014.
18   Adam Withnall, "Cartier Boss with $7.5bn Fortune Says Prospect of the Poor Rising Up 'Keeps Him Awake at Night,'" *Independent*, June 9, 2015.

unemployment, you can try to buy off the masses for a while, and then you can try to repress them by force. But so long as immiserated hordes exist, there is the danger that one day it may become impossible to hold them at bay. When mass labor has been rendered superfluous, a final solution lurks: the genocidal war of the rich against the poor. The specter of automation rises once again, but in a very different way. Under rentism, it merely tended to make more and more workers superfluous, intensifying the system's tendency toward underemployment and weak demand. An exterminist society can automate and mechanize the process of suppression and extermination, allowing the rulers and their minions to distance themselves from the consequences of their actions.

But is that final move, from repression to outright extermination, really plausible? Such slippages begin first where a class conflict is overlaid with a national one, as in the Israeli occupation of Palestine. At one time, Israel heavily depended on cheap Palestinian labor. But as political economist Adam Hanieh has demonstrated, since the late 1990s these workers have been displaced by migrant laborers from Asia and Eastern Europe.[19] Having thus rendered Palestinians superfluous as workers, Israel is able to give free reign to the more fanatical aspects of Zionism's settler-colonial project. In its 2014 assault on the Gaza Strip, the government made claims of "self-defense" that were almost laughably perfunctory,

---

19   Adam   Hanieh,   "Palestine   in   the   Middle   East: Opposing Neoliberalism and US Power," *Monthly Review*, July 19, 2008.

even as they bombed hospitals, schools, and power plants, indiscriminately killing men, women, and children alike and leveling much of the housing stock. Open calls for genocide came from members of the Israeli parliament; one, Ayelet Shaked, proclaimed that "the entire Palestinian people is the enemy." On this basis she justified the destruction of Gaza as a whole, "including its elderly and its women, its cities and its villages, its property and its infrastructure."[20]

Americans might think themselves immune to such barbarity, despite the political class's almost uniform support for Israel's war on Gaza. But Nobel Peace Prize–winning President Barack Obama already claims the right to kill American citizens without the pretense of due process. His government even uses algorithmic methods to identify targets without necessarily knowing their identities.

In 2012, the *Washington Post* published a story about something called the "disposition matrix."[21] This was the Obama administration's "next-generation targeting list," a sort of spreadsheet of doom used to keep track of all those foreigners marked for anonymous drone assassination as alleged terrorists. The story was full of chilling comments from officials. One of them remarks that a killer drone is "like your lawn mower": no matter how many terrorists you kill, "the grass is going to grow back." To streamline the process of indefinite killing, then, the process is partially automated.

---

20   Michael Lerner, "The New Israeli Government: It's Worse than You Think," *Tikkun*, May 7, 2015.
21   Greg Miller, "Plan for Hunting Terrorists Signals US Intends to Keep Adding Names to Kill Lists," *Washington Post*, October 23, 2012.

The *Post* reports on the development of algorithms for so-called "'signature strikes,' which allow the CIA and [Joint Special Operations Command] to hit targets based on patterns of activity . . . even when the identities of those who would be killed is unclear."[22]

Such actions are supported by a substantial number of Americans. Sadly, this indifference to the deaths of those seen as foreigners or others has long characterized the response to US warmaking. But the exterminist mindset has its echoes domestically as well. In the United States, the willingness to countenance the elimination of unruly surplus populations is tightly intertwined with racism, though it is unquestionably a class phenomenon as well. This can be seen in a prison system that now incarcerates 2 million people, many for nonviolent drug offenses. And it often does so in conditions that Supreme Court Justice Anthony Kennedy called "incompatible with the concept of human dignity," with "no place in civilized society," in his opinion on overcrowding in the California prison system.[23]

The American prison system has long been a way to control the unemployed who get locked away inside while buying off those who remain on the outside. In her analysis of the California prison system, Ruth Wilson Gilmore describes the massive growth of incarceration as the construction of a "golden gulag."[24] Urban youth who lack

22 Ibid.
23 *Brown v. Plata*, 134 S. Ct., No. 09-1233 (2011).
24 Ruth Wilson Gilmore, *Golden Gulag: Prisons, Surplus, Crisis, and*

social services and jobs are ruthlessly targeted by police, locked up for long terms under draconian drug laws and California's "three strikes" provision. The resulting explosion in prison construction, meanwhile, provides jobs in rural areas of the state with depressed economies. With agricultural work automated or shifted to ultra-low-wage migrant labor, and manufacturing jobs lost to deindustrialization, prison work has become among the last remaining well-paid labor in these places.

Prison sentencing can even be offloaded onto algorithms, the better to allow administrators to deny their active role in constructing these warehouses of misery. At least twenty US states now use so-called "evidence-based sentencing." The name sounds innocuous—who could oppose the use of evidence? Richard Redding, a University of Virginia law professor and advocate of the method, goes so far as to claim that it "may even be unethical" to use sentencing techniques that are not "transparent" and "entirely rational."[25] But the factors that can go into an evidence-based sentence, by Redding's own account, include not just crimes a person has committed, but those they might commit in the future—the "risk factors" and "criminogenic needs" that "increase the likelihood of recidivism." At this point these models of "future crime risk" start to come uncomfortably close to the

Opposition in Globalizing California, Oakland: University of California Press, 2006.

25   Richard E. Redding, "Evidence-Based Sentencing: The Science of Sentencing Policy and Practice," *Chapman Journal of Criminal Justice* 1: 1, 2009, pp. 1–19.

dystopia of the Philip K. Dick story (and later Tom Cruise movie) *The Minority Report*, in which a "Precrime" division arrests people for crimes they have not yet committed.

Today even some on the right are questioning mass incarceration, sometimes simply on budgetary grounds. But barring any effort to actually provide for either prisoners or the workers who benefit from the prison boom, what is to become of all these surplus populations? Sometimes, those who make it to prison are the lucky ones. Steeped in a culture that is quick to resort to violence, police forces routinely maim and kill those suspected of minor crimes or no crime at all. The brutality of the police is not new, but two things have changed: they have become more militarized and more heavily armed, while the Internet and the ubiquity of video recording equipment has made documentation of their behavior easier.

Radley Balko has described the militarization of the police as the emergence of the "warrior cop."[26] Police increasingly dress in military style and think in military terms. SWAT teams, heavily armed paramilitary units that were originally promoted as a response to high-level threats, are now deployed as a matter of routine. A few hundred SWAT raids per year were conducted across the United States in the 1970s; now there are 100 to 150 every *day*. Often these raids are responding to minor crimes like marijuana possession or gambling. And they can be performed without a warrant,

---

26   Radley Balko, *Rise of the Warrior Cop: The Militarization of America's Police Forces*, New York: Public Affairs, 2013.

under the guise of being "administrative searches" such as
license inspections. A few videos of these raids can be found
on the Internet, and they convey the surreal horror of a heavily armed battalion storming someone's house over a few
ounces of pot.

The result is a steady stream of dead and injured suspects
and their family members—or nonsuspects, in the frequent
scenario where the SWAT team invades the wrong house, as
Balko documents at great length. He cites raids like the one
in 2003, when fifty-seven-year-old government employee
Alberta Spruill died of a heart attack after the New York
Police Department threw a "flash-bang" grenade into what
they thought was the apartment of a drug dealer, based only
on an anonymous tip.

Even when they have the right address, militarized police
responses can cause chaos and destruction that even the
people who called the police in the first place never intended.
The 2015 documentary *Peace Officer* tells the story of Dub
Lawrence, a former Utah county sheriff who became a police
critic after his son-in-law was shot by a SWAT team officer
during a standoff that was originally precipitated by a domestic violence call from his girlfriend.[27]

At the street level, too, the threat of police violence is
constant, especially for the black and brown. In July 2014,
New York City resident Eric Garner died after being
placed in a chokehold by officers, for the suspected crime

---

27   Karen Foshay, "When the SWAT Team You Founded Kills Your
Son-in-Law," Al Jazeera America, March 19, 2015.

of selling untaxed loose cigarettes. His death provoked an uproar in part because the incident was caught on a cell phone camera, but also because it brought attention to something that is all too routine. Soon after, Mike Brown was shot down in the streets of Ferguson, Missouri, giving more fuel to a national movement. Although exact details of the encounter are disputed, all agree that Brown was unarmed and that the officer who shot him started a confrontation over the grave crime of walking in the street. These events echoed many similar incidents around the country, an unceasing drumbeat of violence over the years. In Oakland, for example, there was the police execution of Oscar Grant. After being detained by a transit officer in connection with reports of fighting on a BART train, a bystander's cell phone video showed the officer shouting racial epithets at Grant and then shooting him while he was restrained and face down on the platform. This touched off a protest movement that was an important precursor to Occupy Oakland.

Recent police militarization has its roots in the social upheavals of the 1960s, when the state sought to repress the black freedom and anti-war movements. And the transformation of the police into something akin to an occupying army is inseparable from the history of American imperialism and warmaking abroad, because it is both a literal and figurative case of bringing the war home. Historian Julilly Kohler-Hausmann describes the intersection of these struggles with Vietnam itself, with the imagery of "urban jungles" contributing to "widespread social acceptance of the idea that urban police were engaged in warlike sieges in poor communities."[28] The process of militarization has accelerated in the era of the "war on terror," as not just imagery but weapons flow from the battlefield to the homefront.

More than a diffuse cultural shift, militarized policing should be understood as a conscious state strategy, with the federal government using anti-terrorism as a pretext to make local police more like soldiers. Many police officers are themselves veterans, hardened to civilian deaths by their experiences in places like Iraq and Afghanistan. The US government encourages the transition of soldiers into law enforcement agents through its Community Oriented Policing Services (COPS) program, by prioritizing grants to agencies that hire veterans. Meanwhile, the technology they use—the massive armored fighting vehicles that now grace the streets of even small towns—are repurposed military equipment. The US Department of Homeland Security hands out "anti-terrorism" grants with which police departments large and small can purchase such equipment. Other agencies can acquire similar gear for free, by participating in the Department of Defense's 1033 program, which distributes surplus military equipment freed up by troop withdrawals in Iraq and Afghanistan.[29]

28   Julilly Kohler-Hausmann, "Militarizing the Police: Officer Jon Burge's Torture and Repression in the 'Urban Jungle,' " in Stephen Hartnett, ed., *Challenging the Prison-Industrial Complex: Activism, Arts, and Educational Alternatives*, Urbana: University of Illinois Press, 2010, pp. 43–71.

29   American Civil Liberties Union Foundation, *War Comes Home: The Excessive Militarization of American Policing*, ACLU.org, June 2014.

The result is absurdities like the delivery of a Mine-Resistant Ambush Protected (MRAP) vehicle to High Springs, Florida, population 5,350.[30] These heavily armored, tanklike vehicles were originally used to protect soldiers from the explosives of Iraqi and Afghan insurgents, who are generally thought to be uncommon in central Florida. Perhaps it is unsurprising, then—or perhaps it is a rare example of police sanity—that the police chief of High Springs reported that he had not used the MRAP in the year since receiving it and was hoping to transfer it to another agency. But other departments are happy to roll out the tanks and body armor, as we saw in the images from Ferguson. In a remarkably short time, we've become used to these images, which recall Paul Verhoeven's 1987 movie *Robocop*, a movie that, at the time, was intended as an absurdly over-the-top dystopian depiction of a militarized near-future Detroit.

The warrior cop is not merely a danger to individual train riders and cigarette hawkers, illegal gamblers or occasional pot smokers. Their fate is tied to the fate of political mobilization, as can be seen in the United States and around the world. Mass protest everywhere is already violently repressed, and not just in states like Egypt or China that are popularly regarded as authoritarian. A 2013 report from the International Network of Civil Liberties Organizations documents the widespread "use of lethal

---

30 Paulina Firozi, "Police Forces Pick Up Surplus Military Supplies," *USA Today*, June 15, 2014.

and deadly force in response to largely peaceful gatherings seeking to express social and political viewpoints," in places ranging from Canada to Egypt to Kenya to South Africa to the United States.[31] The crackdown on the Occupy movement was one example of this, a show of force by squads of armored cops in cities across the country. Meanwhile the surveillance-state techniques revealed by former National Security Agency whistleblower Edward Snowden and others show just how powerful are the state's tools for repressing dissent and monitoring the activities of activists.

In this context, it becomes easier to envision the slippage from inhuman prisons, violent police crackdowns, and occasional summary executions to more systematic forms of elimination. Algorithmic targeting, combined with the increasing power of unmanned combat drones, promises to ease the moral discomfort of mass killing, by distancing those who mobilize violence from their targets. Operators can sit safely in remote silos, piloting their death robots in far-off places. It approaches the world of Orson Scott Card's *Ender's Game*. In that story, a child is recruited to train for a war with a race of aliens. As part of his final training, he participates in a simulation in which he destroys the entire homeworld. It was of course not a simulation; young Ender has actually finished the war by committing genocide. Things in our world may not play out with such literal

---

31   International Network of Civil Liberties Organizations, *Take Back the Streets: Repression and Criminalization of Protest Around the World*, ACLU.org, October 2013.

deceptions, but we can already see how our political and economic elites manage to justify ever-higher levels of misery and death while remaining convinced that they are great humanitarians.

CONCLUSION:
TRANSITIONS AND PROSPECTS

This work is not, I have emphasized, an exercise in futurism; I don't aim to predict the precise course of social development. Not only do such predictions have a terrible performance record, they produce an aura of inevitability that encourages us to sit back and passively accept our destiny. The reason there are four futures, and not just one, is because nothing happens automatically. It's up to us to determine the way forward.

Climate justice activists are currently fighting for socialist rather than exterminist solutions to climate change, even if they wouldn't put it that way. And those who are fighting for access to knowledge, against strict intellectual property in everything from seeds to music, are struggling to hold off a rentist dystopia and keep the dream of communism alive. To cover those movements in the detail they deserve would require volumes of their own. So rather than attempt an impossible summary, I'll close with some thoughts about the complexities that arise when we think about the four futures not just as ideals or self-contained utopias, but as the objects of dynamic and ongoing political projects.

For anyone of a left-wing, egalitarian bent, it's easy to say that rentism and exterminism represent the side of evil, and socialism and communism, the hopes of the good. That might be adequate if we conceive of those ideal societies only as destinations or as slogans to put on our banners. But none of these model societies are meant to represent something that could be implemented overnight, in a complete transformation of current social relations. Indeed, probably none of them is possible at all in a pure form; history is simply too messy for that, and real societies exceed the parameters of any theoretical model.

Which means that we should be particularly concerned with the road leading toward these utopias and dystopias, rather than the precise nature of the final destination. Especially because the path that leads to utopia is not necessarily itself utopian.

In Chapter 1, I suggested a particularly fanciful and utopian way to a utopian destination: the "capitalist road to communism" in which the universal basic income lubricates the slide into full communism. But that transition would entail dethroning the ultrarich elite that currently dominates our politics and economics alike. The limited historical experience with actual basic income programs suggests that the rich are unlikely to stand by while their wealth and power wither away, and so there will be difficult struggles.

Consider, for example, the pilot project that was run in 2008 and 2009 in Otjivero-Omitara, Namibia. For two

years, everyone in the village received a monthly payment
of one hundred Namibia dollars (about US$13). In human
terms, even such a minimal basic income was a great success:
school attendance soared, child malnourishment plum-
meted, and even crime declined. But that was of little
concern to the white farmers who made up the local elite.
They insisted, against all evidence, that the basic income
had led to crime and alcoholism. Dirk Haarmann, an economist and theologian who helped implement the basic
income project, speculates that they were "afraid that the
poor will gain some influence and deprive the rich, white 20
percent of the population of some of their power."[1] And
perhaps, more immediately, they were concerned that $100
a month will make workers less eager to accept the $2-per-
hour minimum wage for farm labor.

The transition to a world of abundance and equality, then,
is likely to be a tumultuous and conflict-ridden one. If the
rich won't relinquish their privileges voluntarily, they would
have to be expropriated by force, and such struggles can have
dire consequences for both sides. For as Friedrich Nietzsche
said in a famous aphorism, "Beware that, when fighting
monsters, you yourself do not become a monster . . . for
when you gaze long into the abyss, the abyss gazes also into
you."[2] Or as the Communist poet Bertolt Brecht wrote in

1   Dialika Krahe, "A New Approach to Aid: How a Basic Income
Program Saved a Namibian Village," *Spiegel Online International*, August
10, 2009.
2   Friedrich Nietzsche, *Beyond Good and Evil*, New York: Macmillan,
1907, p. 97.

"To Posterity," a revolution against a brutal system could itself brutalize those who participated in it.

Even anger against injustice
Makes the voice grow harsh. Alas, we
Who wished to lay the foundations of kindness
Could not ourselves be kind.[3]

Or as Mao put it in his characteristic blunt style, "a revolution is not a dinner party."[4] In other words, even the most successful and justified revolution has losers and victims.

In a 1962 letter to the economist Paul Baran, the critical theorist Herbert Marcuse remarks that "nobody ever gave a damn about the victims of history."[5] The remark was directed at the hypocrisy of liberals who were eager to moralize about the victims of Soviet Communism but were silent about the massive human cost of capitalism. It's a harsh, perhaps a cruel judgment, and Marcuse himself suggests the need to move beyond it. But it provides an important perspective on the exercise I've undertaken here, by allowing us to see that society's four futures don't fit into neat moral boxes.

That is one danger, that we underestimate the difficulty of the path we must traverse, or that we allow the beauty of our endpoint to license unlimited brutality along the way. But another possibility is that, at journey's end, we forget how

3   Bertolt Brecht, *Poems, 1913–1956*, London: Routledge, 1979.
4   Mao Tse Tung, *Quotations from Mao Tse Tung*, Marxists.org, 1966.
5   Paul Baran and Herbert Marcuse, "The Baran Marcuse Correspondence," *Monthly Review*, March 1, 2014.

arduous the journey was and who we left behind. Walter Benjamin, in his essay "On the Concept of History," talks about the way that historical accounts necessarily tend to empathize with the victors, who are generally the ones who get to write the history. "Those who currently rule are however the heirs of all those who have ever been victorious. Empathy with the victors thus comes to benefit the current rulers every time."[6] But we can also say that even in a society without clear rulers, history will tend to empathize with the survivors; they are, after all, literally the only ones around to write it. Let's revisit, on that note, the residents of our first, communist future. Perhaps they're not at the end of the capitalist road to communism after all, but of a much longer and darker journey through the horrors of exterminism.

Remember exterminism's central problematic: abundance and freedom from work are possible for a minority, but material limits make it impossible to extend that same way of life to everyone. At the same time, automation has rendered masses of workers superfluous. The result is a society of surveillance, repression, and incarceration, always threatening to tip over into one of outright genocide.

But suppose we stare into that abyss? What's left when the "excess" bodies have been disposed of and the rich are finally left alone with their robots and their walled compounds? The combat drones and robot executioners could be decommissioned, the apparatus of surveillance gradually dismantled,

---

6   Walter Benjamin, "On the Concept of History," trans. Dennis Redmond, Marxists.org, 1940.

and the remaining population could evolve past its brutal and dehumanizing war morality and settle into a life of equality and abundance—in other words, into communism.

As a descendant of Europeans in the United States, I have an idea of what that might be like. After all, I'm the beneficiary of a genocide.

My society was founded on the systematic extermination of the North American continent's original inhabitants. Today, the surviving descendants of those earliest Americans are sufficiently impoverished, small in number, and geographically isolated that most Americans can easily ignore them as they go about their lives. Occasionally the survivors force themselves onto our attention. But mostly, while we may lament the brutality of our ancestors, we don't contemplate giving up our prosperous lives or our land. Just as Marcuse said, nobody ever gave a damn about the victims of history.

Zooming out a bit farther, then, the point is that we don't necessarily pick one of the four futures: we could get them all, and there are paths that lead from each one to all of the others.

We have seen how exterminism becomes communism. Communism, in turn, is always subject to counterrevolution, if someone can find a way to reintroduce artificial scarcity and create a new rentist elite. Socialism is subject to this pressure even more severely, since the greater level of shared material hardship increases the impetus for some group to set itself up as the privileged elite and turn the system into an exterminist one.

But short of a civilizational collapse so complete that it cuts us off from our accumulated knowledge and plunges us into a new dark ages, it's hard to see a road that leads back to industrial capitalism as we have known it. That is the other important point of this book. We can't go back to the past, and we can't even hold on to what we have now. Something new is coming—and indeed, in some way, all four futures are already here, "unevenly distributed," in William Gibson's phrase. It's up to us to build the collective power to fight for the futures we want.